CoreCommonStandards.com

Common Core State Standards

Second Grade Activities Common Core Workbook

Grade 2

● Math Standards

Activities that teach every Common Core Standard!

Table of Contents

Mathematics

Answer Key

2

Common Core
State Standards

**Second Grade Activities
Common Core Workbook**

Grade 2

• Math Standards

**Activities that teach every
Common Core Standard!**

Barnyard Math

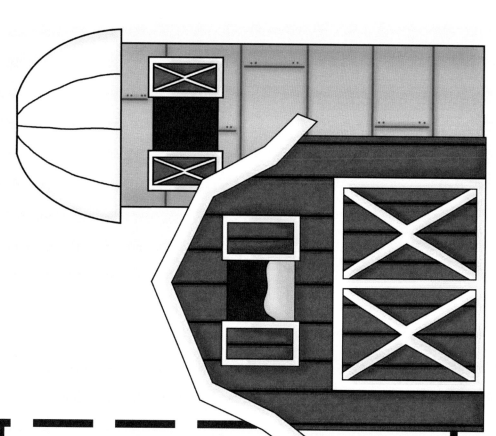

Directions:

Use addition and subtraction within 100 to solve one- and two-step word problems involving situations of adding to, taking from, putting together, taking apart, and comparing, with unknowns in all positions, e.g., by using drawings and equations with a symbol for the unknown number to represent the problem.

Students take turns answering word problem cards using the Draw it! for support. For a correct answer, students get to play an X or O on the Tic-Tac-Toe board.

Laminate the Draw it! for multiple uses.

Students use addition and subtraction to solve one- and two-step word problems and plug in letters to find the answer to the joke "What do you call a grouchy cow?"

Standard: Math| Operations and Algebraic Thinking| 2.OA.1
Graphics by Scrappin Doodles   www.CoreCommonStandards.com

This is a Blank Page

You May Cut Out Resources On Back

This is a Blank Page

Draw It!

Equation:

This is a Blank Page

You May Cut Out Resources On Back

This is a Blank Page

Farmer Joe had 49 cups of food for the pigs. The pigs got into their food & ate 19 cups of food. How much food is left?

The chickens laid 15 eggs in the morning and 19 eggs at night. How many eggs did the chickens lay altogether?

The farm has 24 cows, 13 cows escape out of the pasture. How many cows stay at the farm?

The farmer picked 22 apples, but the cows ate 14 of them. How many does he have left?

A farmer sells 5 cows and 11 pigs. How many animals did he sell?

The farmer built 39 feet of fence on Monday and 41 feet of fence on Tuesday. How many feet of fence did he build?

This is a Blank Page

You May Cut Out Resources On Back

This is a Blank Page

12 Ducks were on the pond, 8 more flew in . How many ducks are on the pond?

www.CoreCommonStandards.com

There were 53 balls of wool at the farm. Anne used 12 balls of wool to make a scarf. How many balls of wool are left?

www.CoreCommonStandards.com

The horses gave 4 boys rides and 8 girls rides. How many rides were given by the horses?

www.CoreCommonStandards.com

35 pigs were rolling in the mud, 14 left to go sunbathing. How many pigs were left in the mud?

www.CoreCommonStandards.com

The farmer feeds the cows 6 cups of feed at breakfast and 6 cups of feed for dinner. How much do they get fed each day?

www.CoreCommonStandards.com

The black cat caught 9 mice and the yellow cat caught 23 mice. How many mice did the cats catch?

www.CoreCommonStandards.com

This is a Blank Page

You May Cut Out Resources On Back

This is a Blank Page

Tic-Tac-Toe

This is a Blank Page

You May Cut Out Resources On Back

This is a Blank Page

Name: _____

	Picture	Equation
O There are some cows playing in the field. 3 cows are by the stream. 2 cows are by the barn. 5 more cows are near the trough. How many cows are playing all together?		
D On the pig there are lots of flies. 7 by his ear, 2 by his tail and 4 by his feet. How many flies are on the pig?		
Y The chicken laid 2 eggs in the morning, 10 eggs at lunchtime and then, 4 eggs more at night. How many eggs did the chicken lay today?		
M The farmer sold 20 ears of corn to one customer and 14 ears of corn to another customer. How many ears of corn did he sell?		

What do you call a grouchy cow?

$$\overline{34} \ \overline{10} \ \overline{10} \ - \ \overline{13} \ \overline{16} \ !$$

Standard: Math| Operations and Algebraic Thinking| 2.OA.1   www.CoreCommonStandards.com

This is a Blank Page

You May Cut Out Resources On Back

This is a Blank Page

Lets workout our brain!
Mental Math!

Directions:

Fluently add and subtract within 20 using mental strategies. By end of Grade 2, know from memory all sums of two one-digit numbers.

Adding: Students shuffle the cards and lay them face down in the center. Flip over a card so that it is face up. The first player to say out loud the number to make the card equal twenty gets the card. The player who has the most cards is the winner.

Subtracting: Students shuffle and deal the deck of cards between 2 players. Each player lays their cards face down. At the same time, both players turn the top card face up in the center. The first player to say out loud the answer to the subtraction problem (big number – small number) gets the two cards. The player who has the most cards is the winner.

Standard: Math| Operations and Algebraic Thinking| 2.OA.2
Graphics by Scrappin Doodles   www.CoreCommonStandards.com

17

This is a Blank Page

You May Cut Out Resources On Back

This is a Blank Page

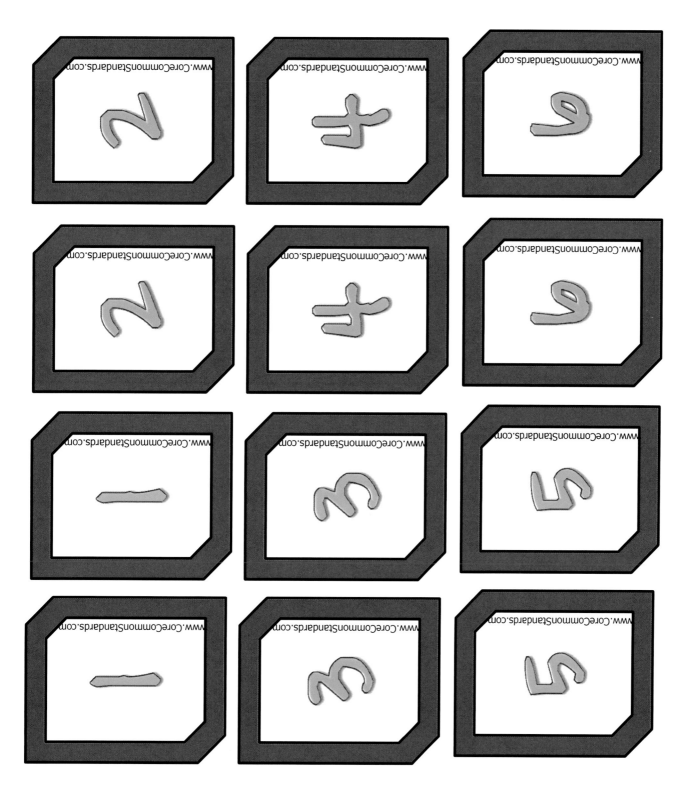

This is a Blank Page

You May Cut Out Resources On Back

This is a Blank Page

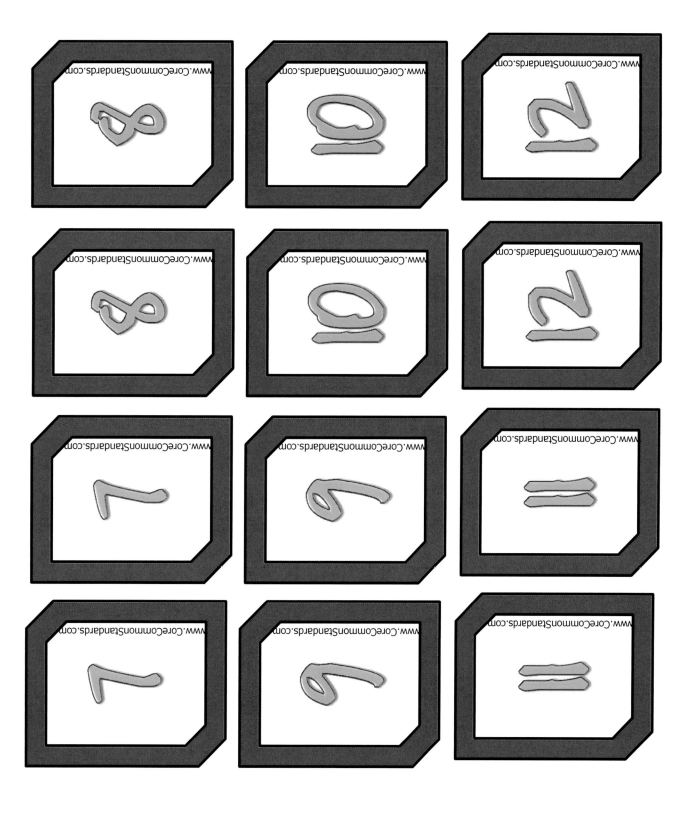

This is a Blank Page

You May Cut Out Resources On Back

This is a Blank Page

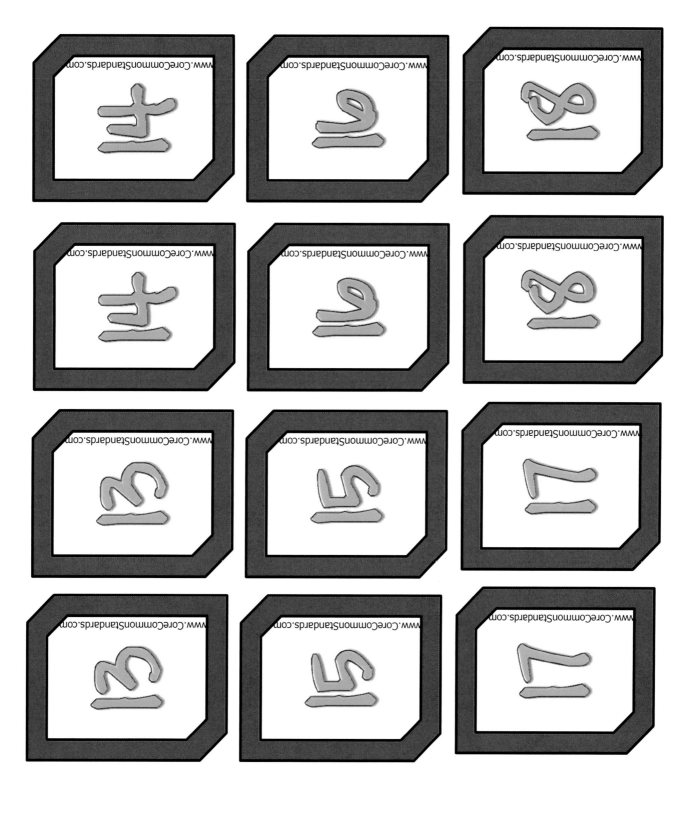

This is a Blank Page

You May Cut Out Resources On Back

This is a Blank Page

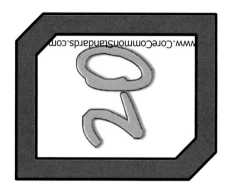

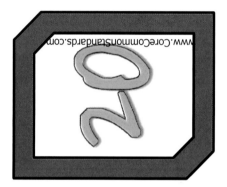

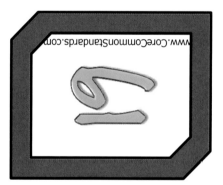

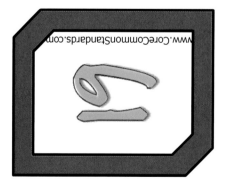

This is a Blank Page

You May Cut Out Resources On Back

This is a Blank Page

ODD OR EVEN?

Directions:

Determine whether a group of objects (up to 20) has an odd or even number of members, e.g., by pairing objects or counting them by 2s; write an equation to express an even number as a sum of two equal addends.

Students will sort the cards into odd and even categories. Then, students can continue practicing determining if a number is odd or even using the Odd and Even Apple Sheet.

Standard: Math| Operations & Algebraic Thinking| 2.OA.3
Clipart by Scrappin' Doodles and clipart.com www.CoreCommonStandards.com

This is a Blank Page

You May Cut Out Resources On Back

This is a Blank Page

EVEN numbers

8
6
4
2

The numbers in the ONES place will have a partner if the number is EVEN!

Standard: Math| Operations & Algebraic Thinking| 2.OA.3   www.CoreCommonStandards.com

This is a Blank Page

You May Cut Out Resources On Back

This is a Blank Page

ODD numbers

9 7 5 3 1

The numbers in the ONES place will not have a partner if the number is ODD!

Standard: Math| Operations & Algebraic Thinking| 2.OA.3   www.CoreCommonStandards.com

This is a Blank Page

You May Cut Out Resources On Back

This is a Blank Page

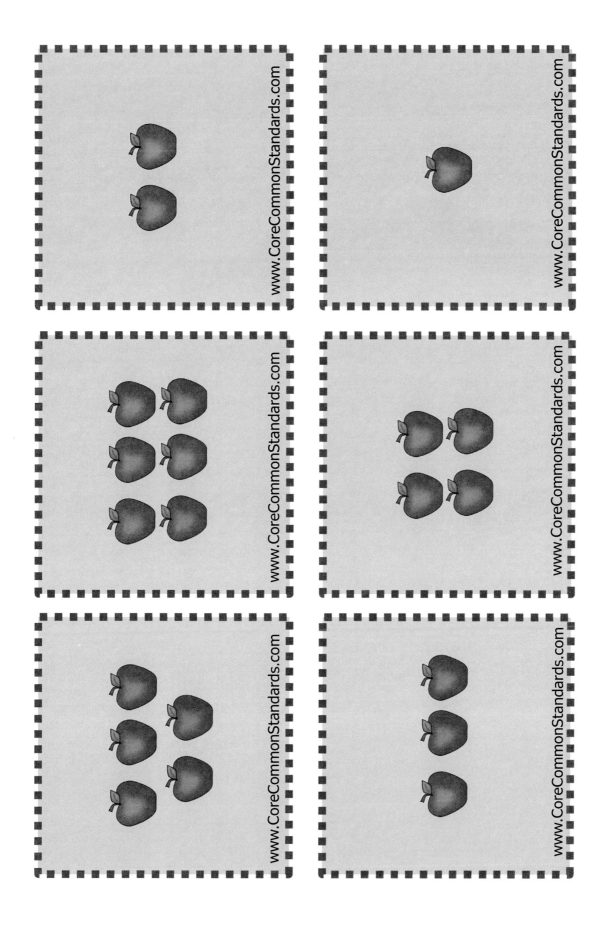

This is a Blank Page

You May Cut Out Resources On Back

This is a Blank Page

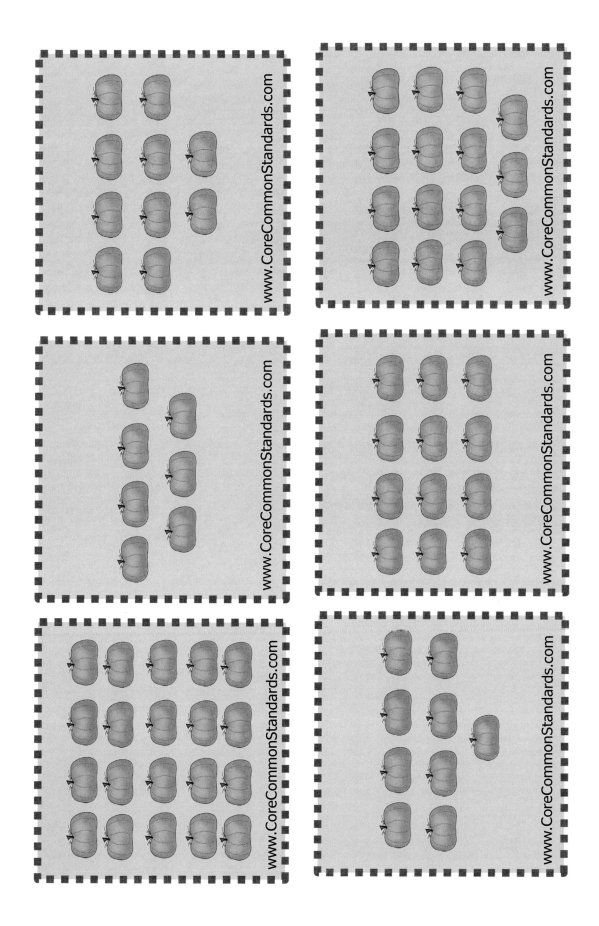

This is a Blank Page

You May Cut Out Resources On Back

This is a Blank Page

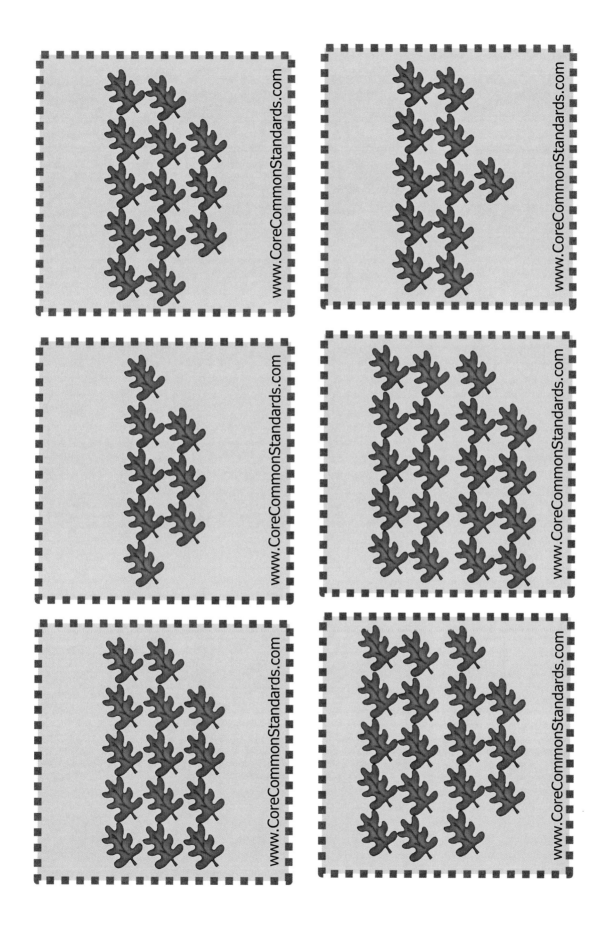

This is a Blank Page

You May Cut Out Resources On Back

This is a Blank Page

odd **numbers**

even **numbers**

This is a Blank Page

You May Cut Out Resources On Back

This is a Blank Page

Name _____

Directions: Color the odd apples brown and the even apples red.

Standard: Math| Operations & Algebraic Thinking| 2.OA.3

www.CoreCommonStandards.com

This is a Blank Page

You May Cut Out Resources On Back

This is a Blank Page

Sweet rectangular arrays

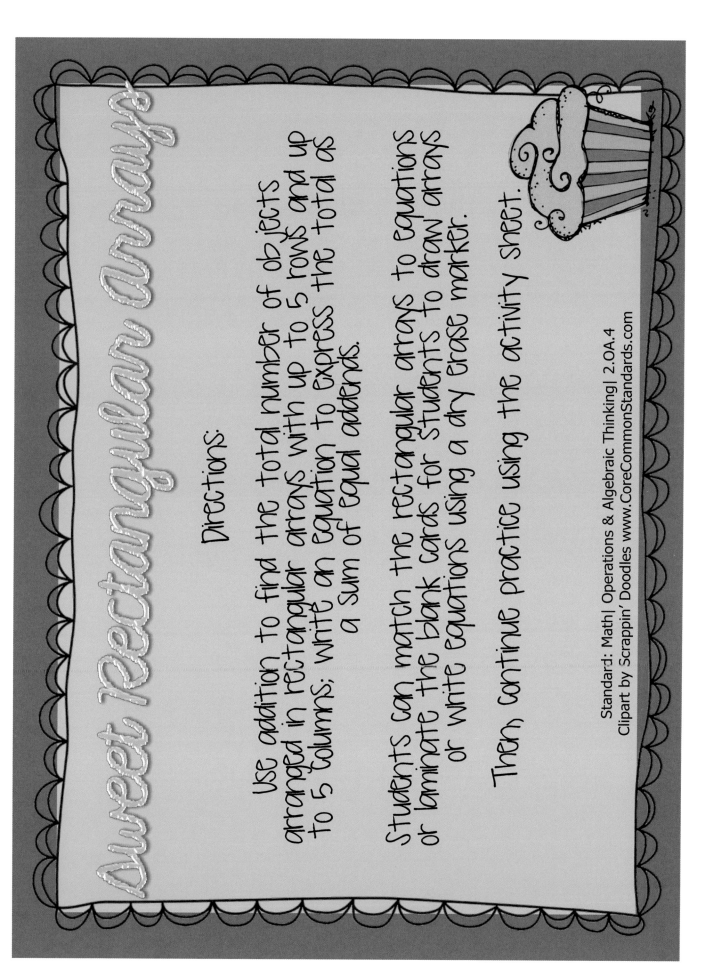

Directions:

Use addition to find the total number of objects arranged in rectangular arrays with up to 5 rows and up to 5 columns; write an equation to express the total as a sum of equal addends.

Students can match the rectangular arrays to equations or laminate the blank cards for students to draw arrays or write equations using a dry erase marker.

Then, continue practice using the activity sheet.

Standard: Math| Operations & Algebraic Thinking| 2.OA.4
Clipart by Scrappin' Doodles www.CoreCommonStandards.com

This is a Blank Page

You May Cut Out Resources On Back

This is a Blank Page

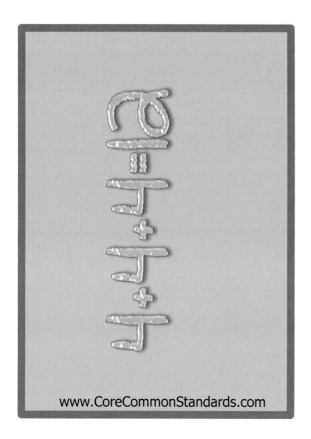

www.CoreCommonStandards.com

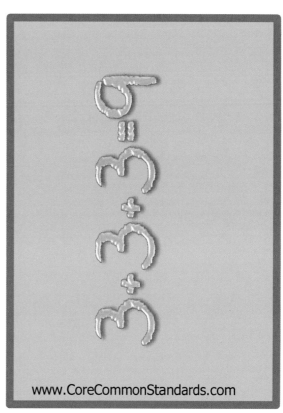

www.CoreCommonStandards.com

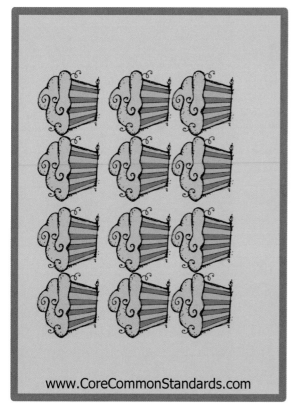

www.CoreCommonStandards.com

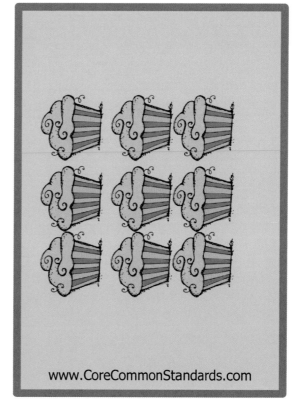

www.CoreCommonStandards.com

This is a Blank Page

You May Cut Out Resources On Back

This is a Blank Page

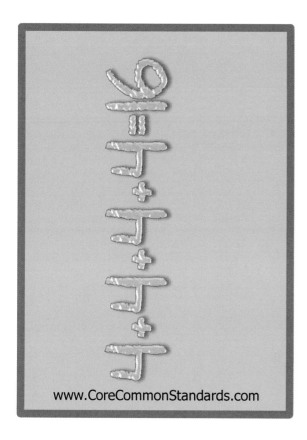

1 + 1 + 1 + 1 + 1 + 1 = 6

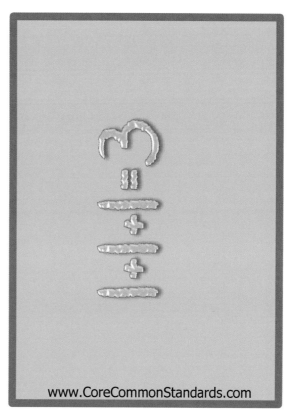

1 + 1 + 1 = 3

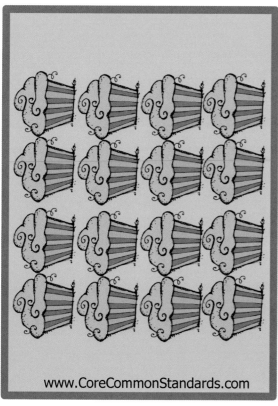

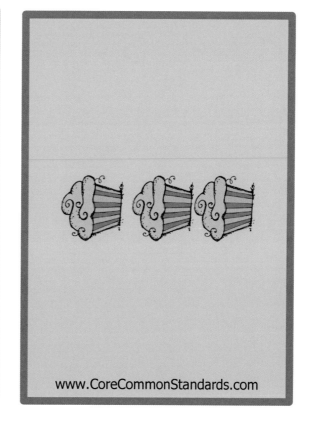

This is a Blank Page

You May Cut Out Resources On Back

This is a Blank Page

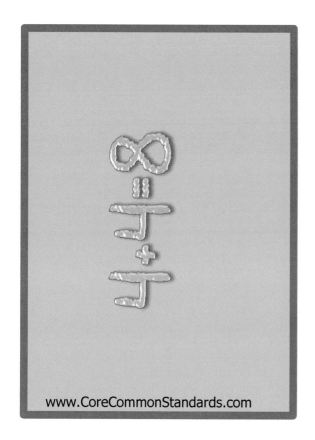

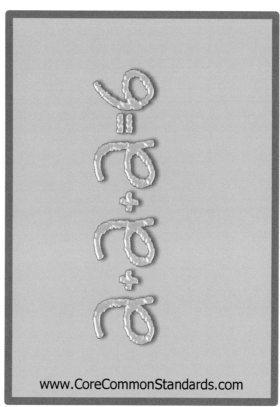

www.CoreCommonStandards.com

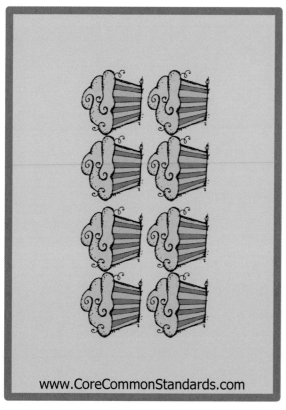

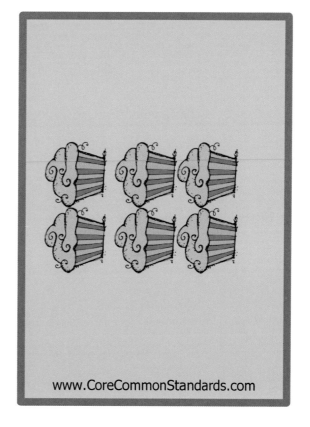

www.CoreCommonStandards.com

This is a Blank Page

You May Cut Out Resources On Back

This is a Blank Page

5 + 5 + 5 = 15

8 + 8 + 8 + 8 + 8 = 8

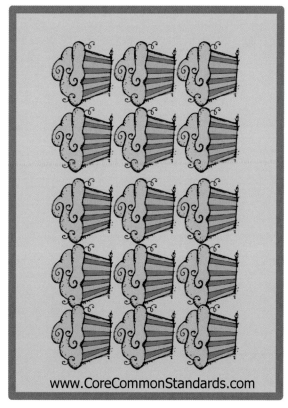

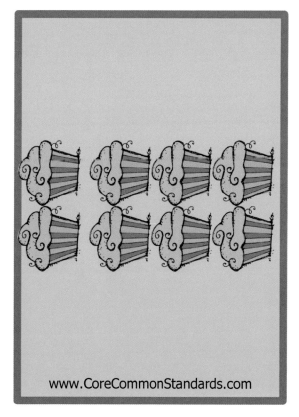

This is a Blank Page

You May Cut Out Resources On Back

This is a Blank Page

www.CoreCommonStandards.com

www.CoreCommonStandards.com

www.CoreCommonStandards.com

www.CoreCommonStandards.com

This is a Blank Page

You May Cut Out Resources On Back

This is a Blank Page

Name: _____

Picture	Equation
	$4+4=8$
	$2+2+2+2+2=10$
	$3+3+3=9$

Standard: Math| Operations & Algebraic Thinking| 2.OA.4

ww.CoreCommonStandards.com

This is a Blank Page

You May Cut Out Resources On Back

This is a Blank Page

LET'S MAKE A NUMBER!

Directions:

Understand that the three digits of a three-digit number represent amounts of hundreds, tens, and ones; e.g., 706 equals 7 hundreds, 0 tens, and 6 ones.

Students shuffle and deal each player 6 number cards. Students each make the highest 3 digit number using their number cards. After each round, students draw 3 more cards.

Record your winning number on your score card and the first one to five wins! Laminate score cards for multiple uses!

Standard: Math| Number & Operations in Base Ten| 2.NBT.1
Clipart by Scrappin' Doodles www.CoreCommonStandards.com

This is a Blank Page

You May Cut Out Resources On Back

This is a Blank Page

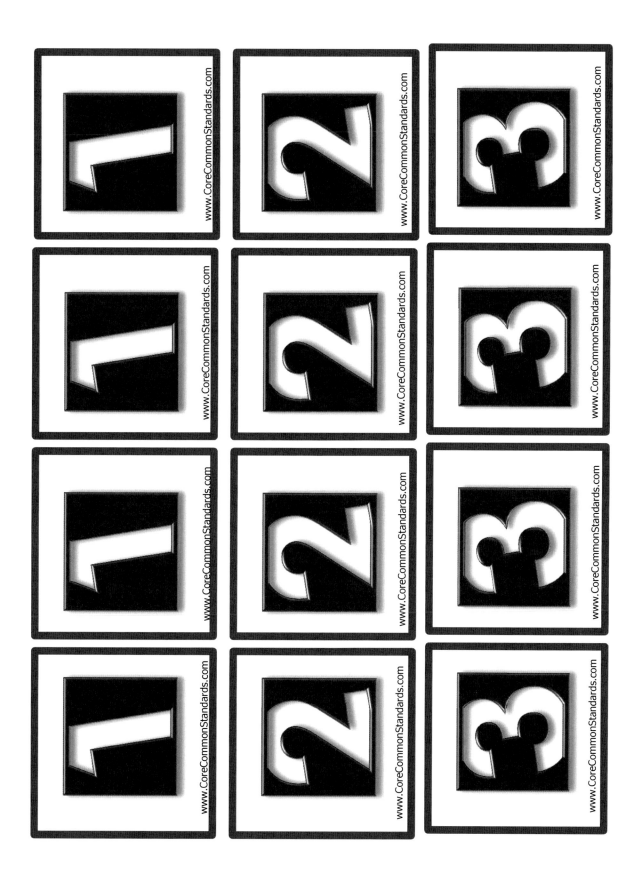

This is a Blank Page

You May Cut Out Resources On Back

This is a Blank Page

This is a Blank Page

You May Cut Out Resources On Back

This is a Blank Page

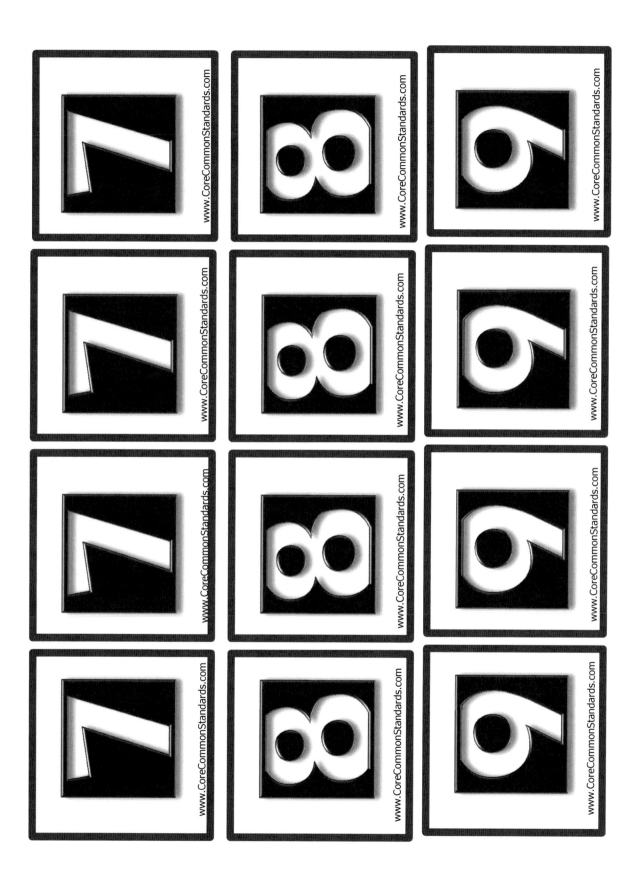

www.CoreCommonStandards.com

This is a Blank Page

You May Cut Out Resources On Back

This is a Blank Page

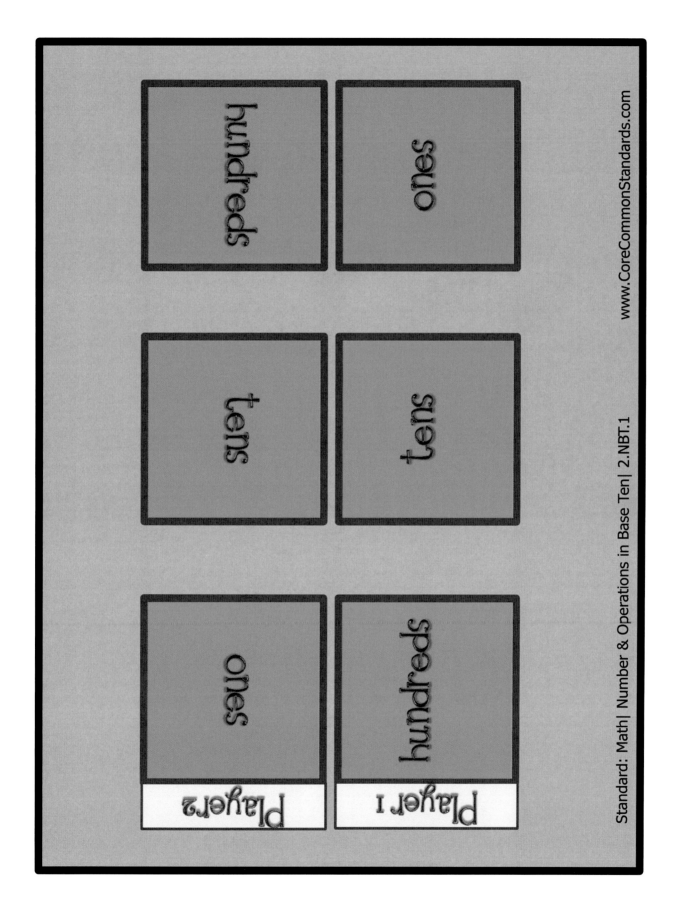

Standard: Math| Number & Operations in Base Ten| 2.NBT.1

www.CoreCommonStandards.com

This is a Blank Page

You May Cut Out Resources On Back

This is a Blank Page

Score Card

www.CoreCommonStandards.com

Score Card

www.CoreCommonStandards.com

This is a Blank Page

You May Cut Out Resources On Back

This is a Blank Page

Skip Counting with Apples

Directions:
Count within 1000; skip-count by 5s, 10s, and 100s. Cut out the pieces of the puzzle for students to practice skip counting. Then, use the activity sheet for more practice and students can even create their own!

Standard: Math| Number & Operations in Base Ten| 2.NBT.2
Graphics by Scrappin Doodles www.CoreCommonStandards.com

This is a Blank Page

You May Cut Out Resources On Back

This is a Blank Page

980,990, ___,___

555,560,565, ___,___

570,575

950,960,970, ___,___

99,100,101, ___,___

102,103

432,433,434, ___,___

435,436

201,301,401, ___,___

501,601

555,565,575, ___,___

585,595

567,577,587, ___,___

597,607

4,5,6, ___,___

7,8

20,30,40, ___,___

50,60

16,17,18, ___,___

19,20

35,40,45, ___,___

50,55

8,13,18, ___,___

23,28

50,55

This is a Blank Page

You May Cut Out Resources On Back

This is a Blank Page

What comes next?

5	10	15	20	25	30
8	10	12	14	16	18
50	60	70	80	90	100
12	13	14	15	16	17

Make your own!

www.CoreCommonStandards.com

Standard: Math| Number & Operations in Base Ten| 2.NBT.2

This is a Blank Page

You May Cut Out Resources On Back

This is a Blank Page

BLAST OFF WITH NUMBERS!

Directions:

Read and write numbers to 1000 using base-ten numerals, number names, and expanded form.

Match the Number Cards to the Expanded Form and Written Form Cards. There should be 21 piles when you are finished.

Students can continue their practice with the activity sheet.

Standard: Math| Number & Operations in Base Ten| 2.NBT.3
Graphics by Scrappin Doodles   www.CoreCommonStandards.com

This is a Blank Page

You May Cut Out Resources On Back

This is a Blank Page

671

www.CoreCommonStandards.com

600+70+1

www.CoreCommonStandards.com

Six
Hundred
Seventy-one

www.CoreCommonStandards.com

469

www.CoreCommonStandards.com

400+60+9

www.CoreCommonStandards.com

Four
Hundred
Sixty-Nine

www.CoreCommonStandards.com

386

www.CoreCommonStandards.com

300+80+6

www.CoreCommonStandards.com

Three
Hundred
Eighty-Six

www.CoreCommonStandards.com

This is a Blank Page

You May Cut Out Resources On Back

This is a Blank Page

121

100+20+1

One Hundred Twenty-One

298

200+90+8

Two Hundred Ninety-Eight

508

500+8

Five Hundred Eight

This is a Blank Page

You May Cut Out Resources On Back

This is a Blank Page

849

800+40+9

Eight Hundred Forty-Nine

225

200+20+5

Two Hundred Twenty-Five

362

300+60+2

Three Hundred Sixty-Two

This is a Blank Page

You May Cut Out Resources On Back

This is a Blank Page

442	400+40+2	Four Hundred Forty-Two
957	900+50+7	Nine Hundred Fifty-Seven
766	700+60+6	Seven Hundred Sixty-Six

www.CoreCommonStandards.com

This is a Blank Page

You May Cut Out Resources On Back

This is a Blank Page

719

700+10+9

Seven Hundred Nineteen

659

600+50+9

Six Hundred Fifty-Nine

243

200+40+3

Two Hundred Forty-Three

This is a Blank Page

You May Cut Out Resources On Back

This is a Blank Page

330

www.CoreCommonStandards.com

300+30

www.CoreCommonStandards.com

Three
Hundred
Thirty

www.CoreCommonStandards.com

566

www.CoreCommonStandards.com

500+60+6

www.CoreCommonStandards.com

Five
Hundred
Sixty-Six

www.CoreCommonStandards.com

841

www.CoreCommonStandards.com

800+40+1

www.CoreCommonStandards.com

Eight
Hundred
Forty-One

www.CoreCommonStandards.com

This is a Blank Page

You May Cut Out Resources On Back

This is a Blank Page

113

www.CoreCommonStandards.com

100+10+3

www.CoreCommonStandards.com

One Hundred Thirteen

www.CoreCommonStandards.com

680

www.CoreCommonStandards.com

600+80

www.CoreCommonStandards.com

Six Hundred Eighty

www.CoreCommonStandards.com

995

www.CoreCommonStandards.com

900+90+5

www.CoreCommonStandards.com

Nine Hundred Ninety-Five

www.CoreCommonStandards.com

This is a Blank Page

You May Cut Out Resources On Back

This is a Blank Page

Name: _____

Expanded Form	Base-Ten	Word Form
700+ 40+ 3	250	
		Two Hundred Eighty-Two
100+ 20+ 9		Seven Hundred Twenty
	875	
		Six Hundred Ninety-Three

Standard: Math| Number & Operations in Base Ten| 2.NBT.3   www.CoreCommonStandards.com

This is a Blank Page

You May Cut Out Resources On Back

This is a Blank Page

Become a Super Hero by

Comparing Numbers

Directions: Compare two three-digit numbers based on meanings of the hundreds, tens, and ones digits, using >, =, and < symbols to record the results of comparisons.

Cut out the number cards for students to compare numbers by playing War! The player that puts down the largest number wins! If the numbers are EQUAL, it's WAR! Students can record their wins on the activity sheet for assessment.

Standard: Math| Number & Operations in Base Ten| 2.NBT.4   www.CoreCommonStandards.com
Graphics by Scrappin Doodles

This is a Blank Page

You May Cut Out Resources On Back

This is a Blank Page

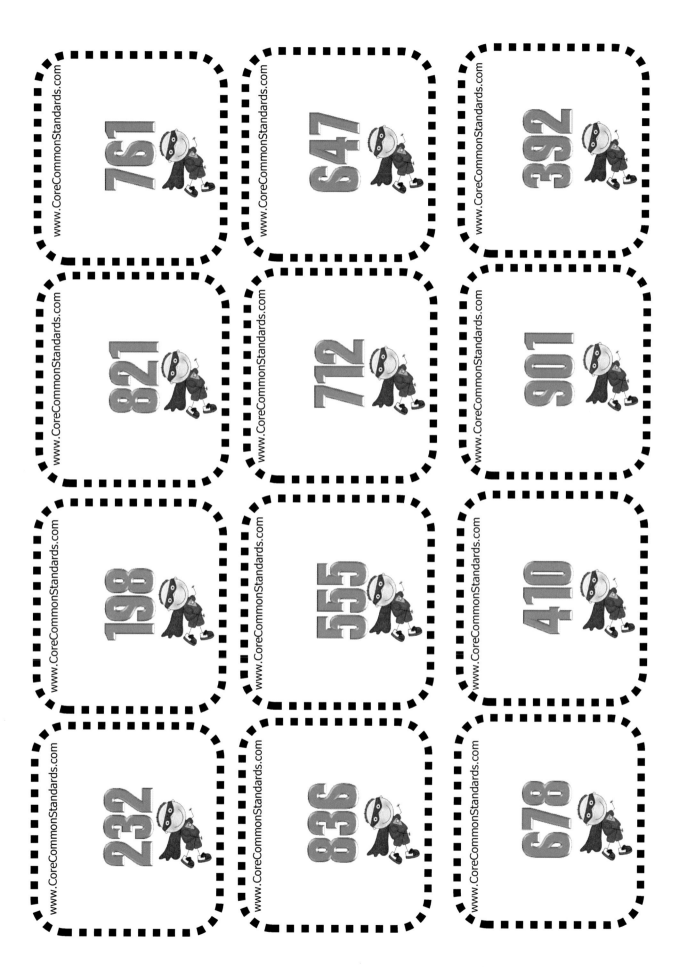

761

647

392

821

712

901

198

555

410

232

836

678

This is a Blank Page

You May Cut Out Resources On Back

This is a Blank Page

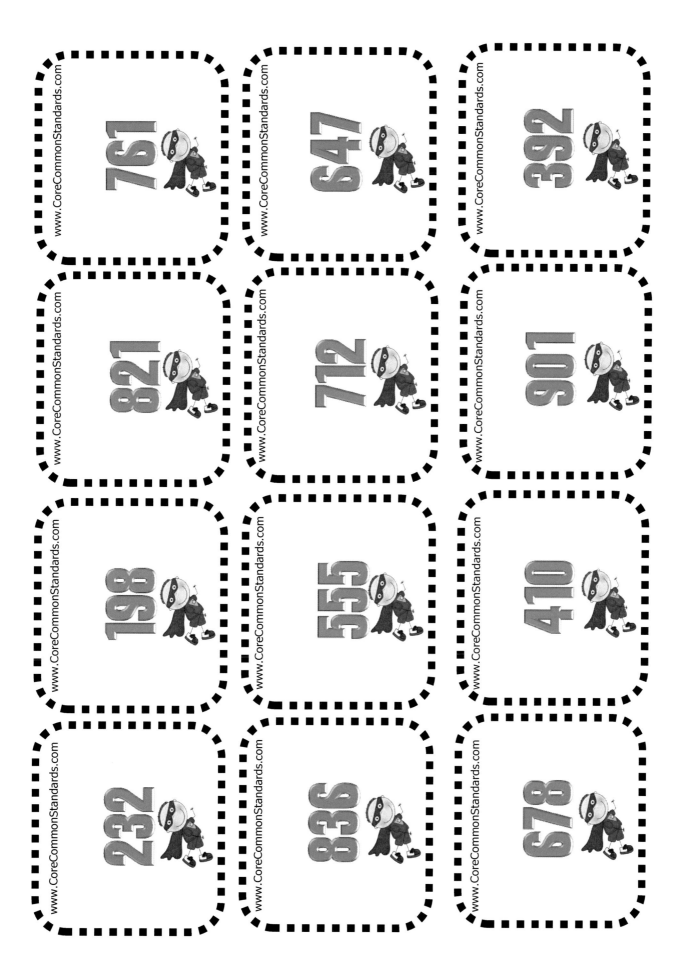

761 www.CoreCommonStandards.com

647 www.CoreCommonStandards.com

392 www.CoreCommonStandards.com

821 www.CoreCommonStandards.com

712 www.CoreCommonStandards.com

901 www.CoreCommonStandards.com

198 www.CoreCommonStandards.com

555 www.CoreCommonStandards.com

410 www.CoreCommonStandards.com

232 www.CoreCommonStandards.com

836 www.CoreCommonStandards.com

678 www.CoreCommonStandards.com

This is a Blank Page

You May Cut Out Resources On Back

This is a Blank Page

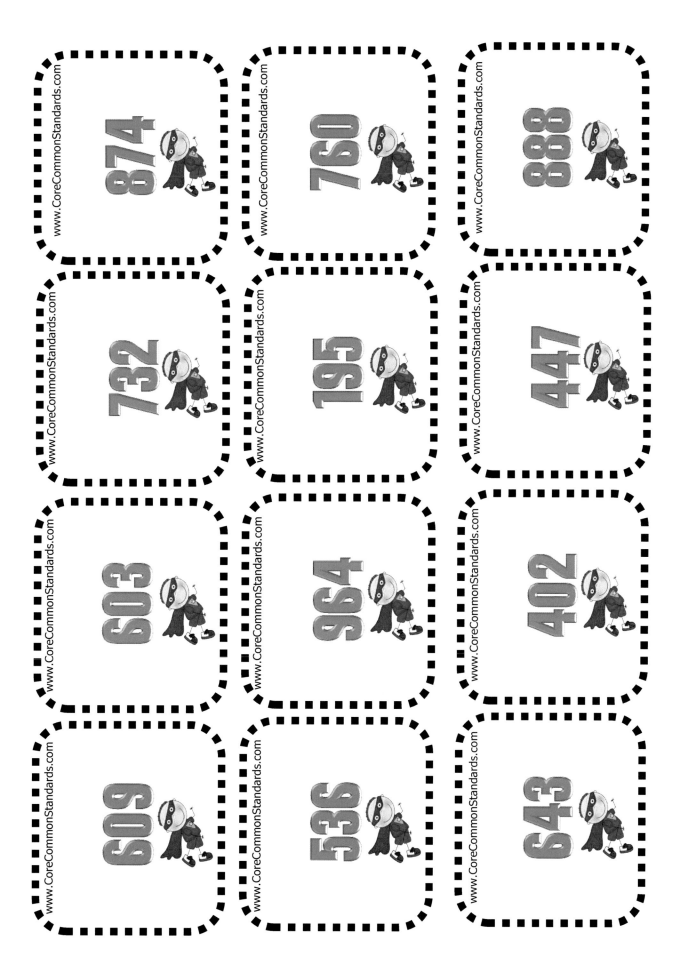

874

760

888

732

195

447

603

964

402

609

536

643

This is a Blank Page

You May Cut Out Resources On Back

This is a Blank Page

This is a Blank Page

You May Cut Out Resources On Back

This is a Blank Page

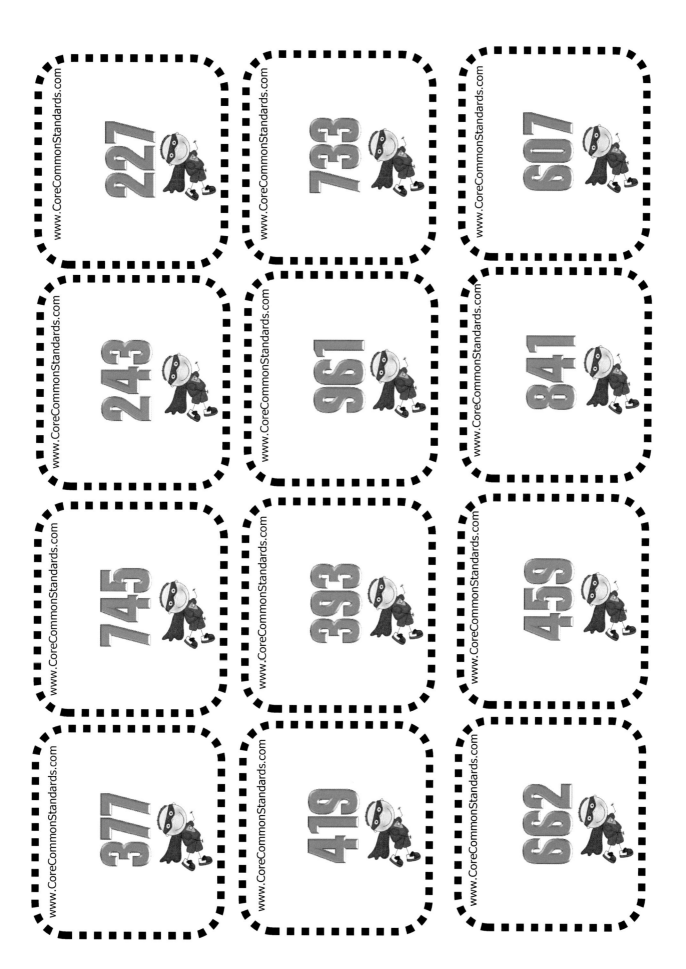

227

733

607

243

961

841

745

393

459

377

419

662

This is a Blank Page

You May Cut Out Resources On Back

This is a Blank Page

207

104

920

182

861

135

217

173

679

583

966

627

This is a Blank Page

You May Cut Out Resources On Back

This is a Blank Page

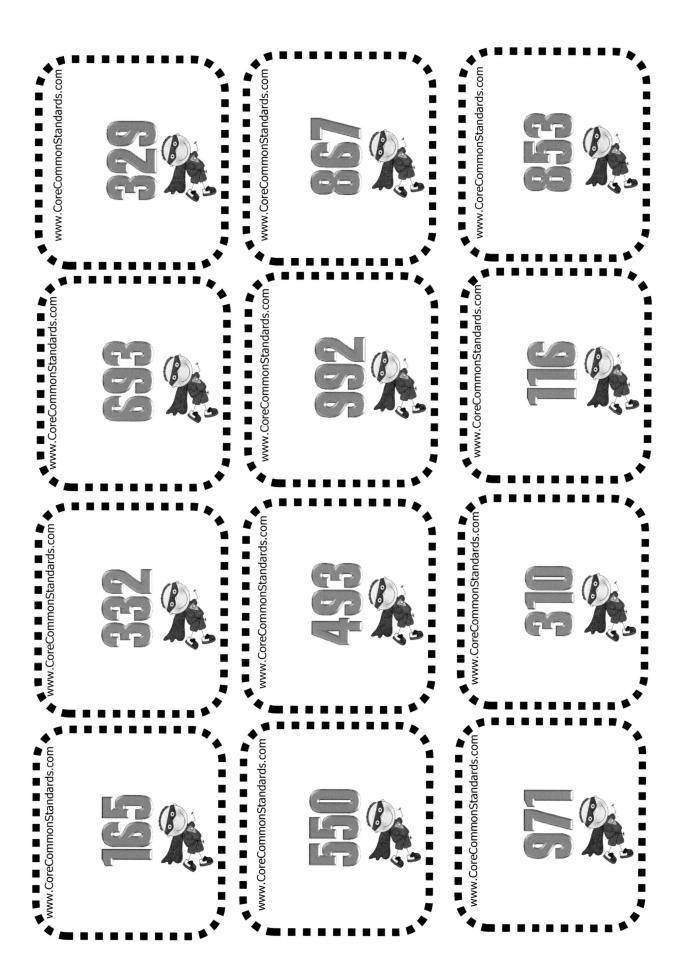

329
867
853
693
992
116
332
493
310
165
550
971

www.CoreCommonStandards.com

This is a Blank Page

You May Cut Out Resources On Back

This is a Blank Page

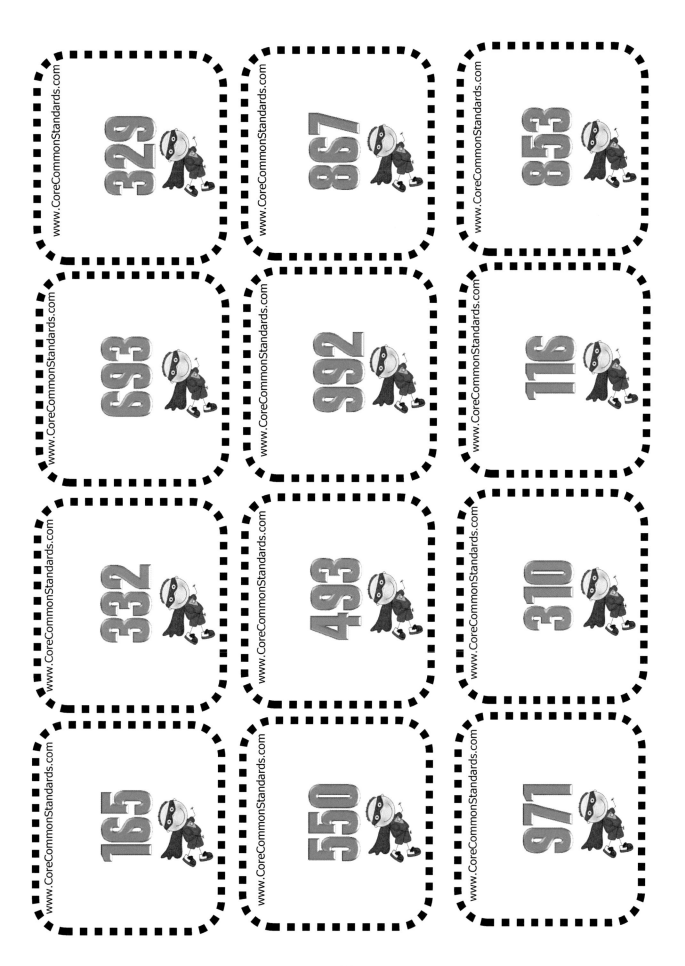

329

867

853

693

992

116

332

493

310

165

550

971

This is a Blank Page

You May Cut Out Resources On Back

This is a Blank Page

Comparing Numbers War

Player 1: _____   **Player 2:** _____

Both players lay down a card. Write the numbers shown on the lines. Then, compare the numbers by placing <, >, or = in the box. The person with the bigger number gets to keep both cards.

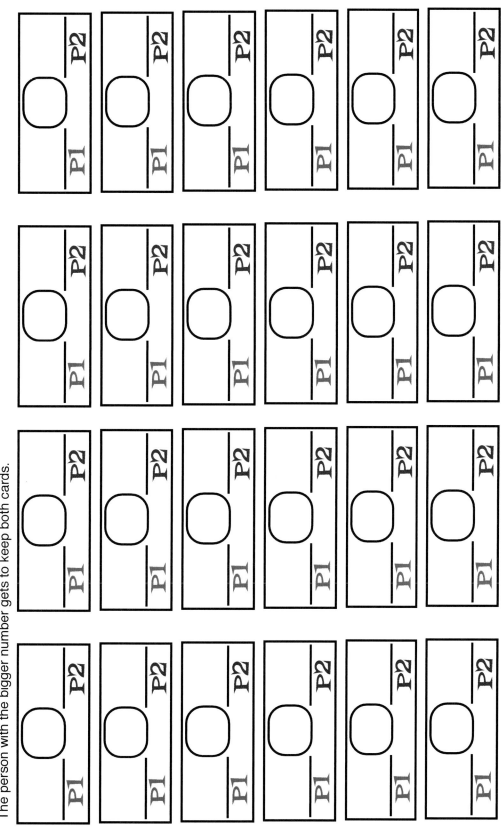

This is a Blank Page

You May Cut Out Resources On Back

This is a Blank Page

Let's go on a TRIP!

Directions:

Fluently add and subtract within 100 using strategies based on place value, properties of operations, and/or the relationship between addition and subtraction.

Cut out and shuffle the item cards. Students flip two cards and add or subtract based on the spinner.

Students record equations on the activity sheet.

Standard: Math| Number & Operations in Base Ten| 2.NBT.5
Clipart by Scrappin' Doodles and clipart.com www.CoreCommonStandards.com

113

This is a Blank Page

You May Cut Out Resources On Back

This is a Blank Page

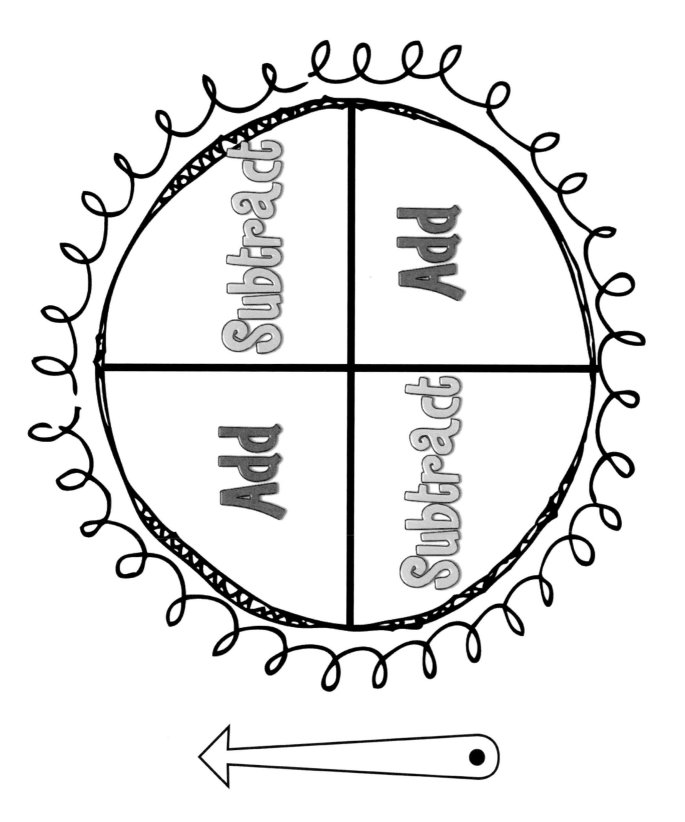

This is a Blank Page

You May Cut Out Resources On Back

This is a Blank Page

Number	Symbol	Number		Answer
			=	
			=	
			=	
			=	
			=	
			=	
			=	
			=	
			=	
			=	
			=	

Standard: Math| Number & Operations in Base Ten| 2.NBT.5   www.CoreCommonStandards.com

This is a Blank Page

You May Cut Out Resources On Back

This is a Blank Page

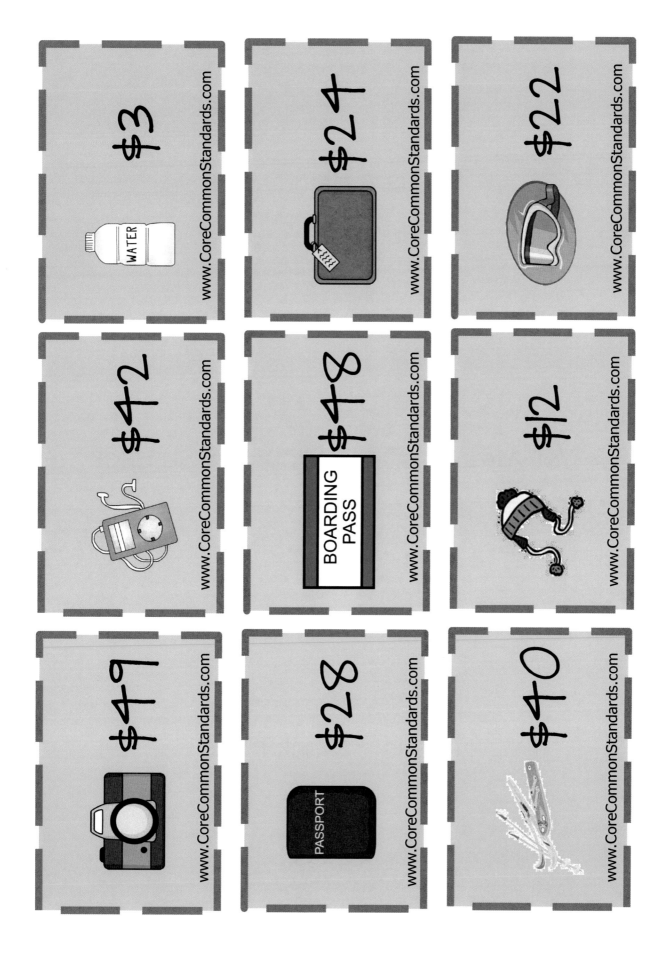

$3

$24

$22

$42

$48

$12

$49

$28

$40

This is a Blank Page

You May Cut Out Resources On Back

This is a Blank Page

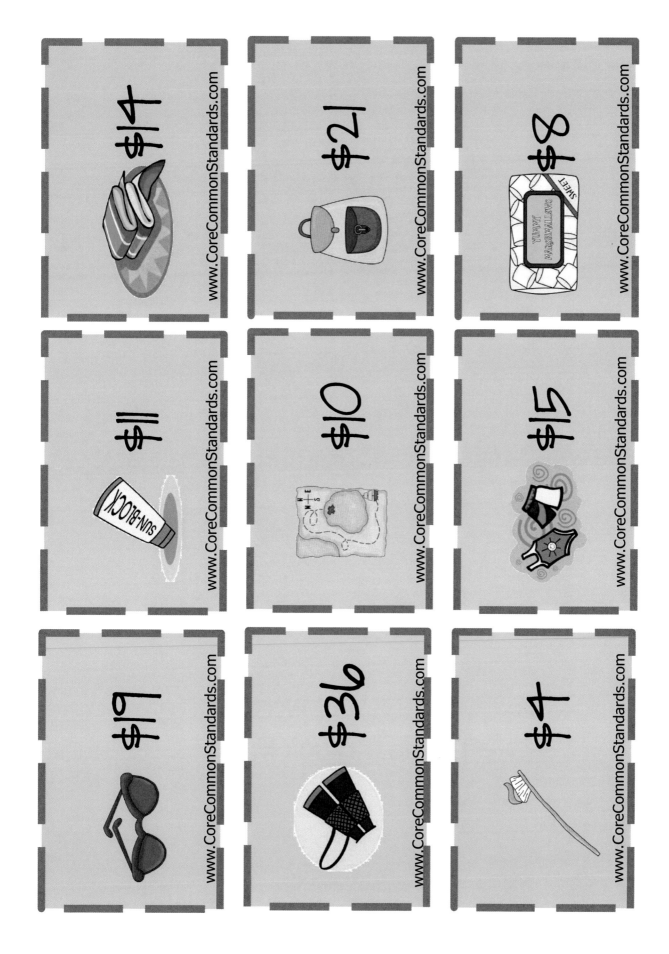

$14

$21

$8

www.CoreCommonStandards.com

www.CoreCommonStandards.com

www.CoreCommonStandards.com

$11

$10

$15

www.CoreCommonStandards.com

www.CoreCommonStandards.com

www.CoreCommonStandards.com

$19

$36

$4

www.CoreCommonStandards.com

www.CoreCommonStandards.com

www.CoreCommonStandards.com

This is a Blank Page

You May Cut Out Resources On Back

This is a Blank Page

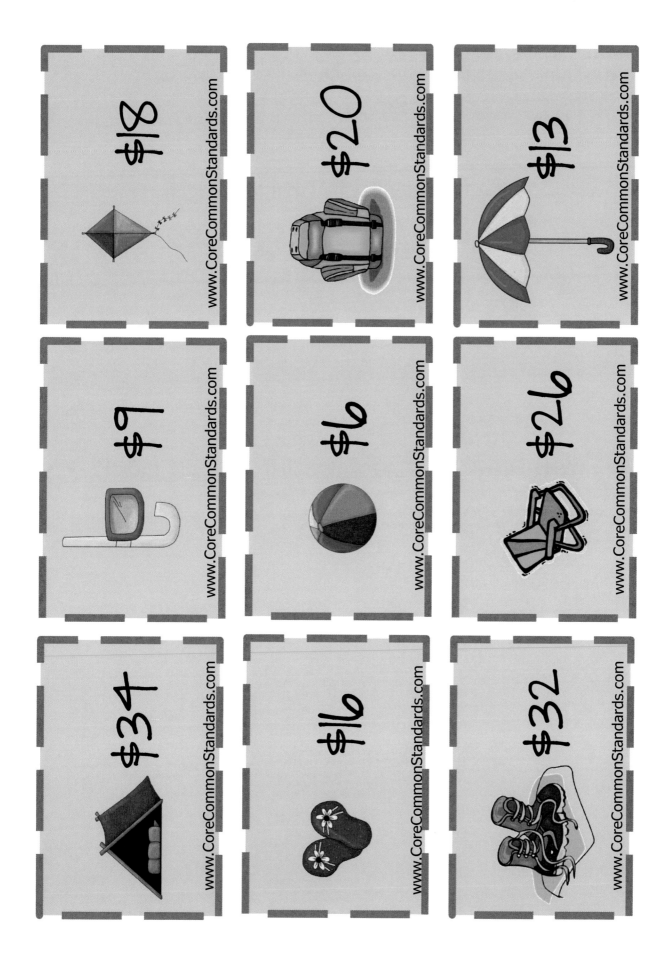

$18

www.CoreCommonStandards.com

$20

www.CoreCommonStandards.com

$13

www.CoreCommonStandards.com

$9

www.CoreCommonStandards.com

$6

www.CoreCommonStandards.com

$26

www.CoreCommonStandards.com

$34

www.CoreCommonStandards.com

$16

www.CoreCommonStandards.com

$32

www.CoreCommonStandards.com

This is a Blank Page

You May Cut Out Resources On Back

This is a Blank Page

Name:

49 + 42 7 ‾‾‾‾	28 + 48 24 ‾‾‾‾	40 + 12 22 ‾‾‾‾
19 + 11 14 ‾‾‾‾	36 + 10 21 ‾‾‾‾	Make your own!

Standard: Math| Number & Operations in Base Ten| 2.NBT.5   www.CoreCommonStandards.com

This is a Blank Page

You May Cut Out Resources On Back

This is a Blank Page

Adding Two-Digit Numbers

$$
\begin{array}{r}
12 \\
32 \\
+\ 24 \\
\hline
\end{array}
$$

Directions:

Add up to four two-digit numbers using strategies based on place value and properties of operations. Choose an Activity Card that shows how many Number Cards to pick. Then, draw that many Number Cards and add them together using the practice worksheet.

Standard: Mathematics | Number and Operations in Base Ten | 2.NBT.6

Graphics by ScrappinDoodles   www.CoreCommonStandards.com

This is a Blank Page

You May Cut Out Resources On Back

This is a Blank Page

Pick 2
Number Cards
And add them together.

www.CoreCommonStandards.com

Pick 3
Number Cards
And add them together.

www.CoreCommonStandards.com

Pick 4
Number Cards
And add them together.

www.CoreCommonStandards.com

Pick 2
Number Cards
And add them together.

www.CoreCommonStandards.com

Pick 3
Number Cards
And add them together.

www.CoreCommonStandards.com

Pick 4
Number Cards
And add them together.

www.CoreCommonStandards.com

This is a Blank Page

You May Cut Out Resources On Back

This is a Blank Page

10
www.CoreCommonStandards.com

11
www.CoreCommonStandards.com

12
www.CoreCommonStandards.com

13
www.CoreCommonStandards.com

14
www.CoreCommonStandards.com

15
www.CoreCommonStandards.com

This is a Blank Page

You May Cut Out Resources On Back

This is a Blank Page

20
www.CoreCommonStandards.com

21
www.CoreCommonStandards.com

22
www.CoreCommonStandards.com

23
www.CoreCommonStandards.com

24
www.CoreCommonStandards.com

25
www.CoreCommonStandards.com

This is a Blank Page

You May Cut Out Resources On Back

This is a Blank Page

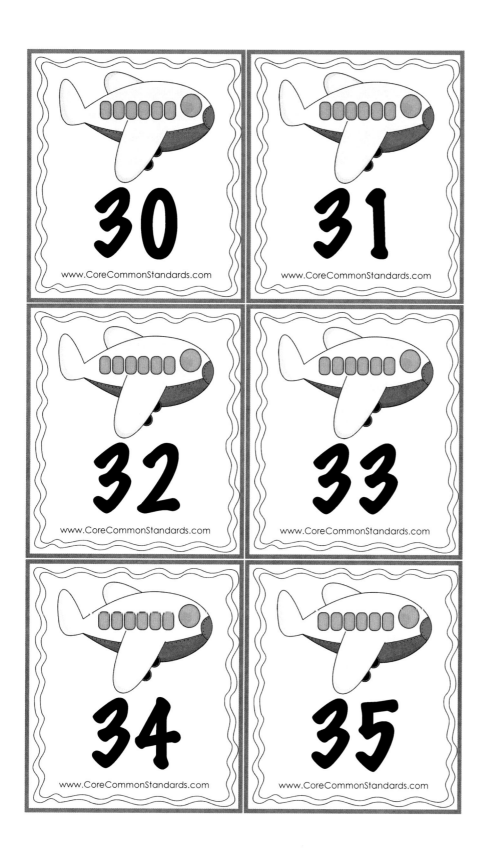

30
www.CoreCommonStandards.com

31
www.CoreCommonStandards.com

32
www.CoreCommonStandards.com

33
www.CoreCommonStandards.com

34
www.CoreCommonStandards.com

35
www.CoreCommonStandards.com

This is a Blank Page

You May Cut Out Resources On Back

This is a Blank Page

40
www.CoreCommonStandards.com

41
www.CoreCommonStandards.com

42
www.CoreCommonStandards.com

43
www.CoreCommonStandards.com

44
www.CoreCommonStandards.com

45
www.CoreCommonStandards.com

This is a Blank Page

You May Cut Out Resources On Back

This is a Blank Page

50 www.CoreCommonStandards.com

51 www.CoreCommonStandards.com

52 www.CoreCommonStandards.com

53 www.CoreCommonStandards.com

54 www.CoreCommonStandards.com

55 www.CoreCommonStandards.com

This is a Blank Page

You May Cut Out Resources On Back

This is a Blank Page

60
www.CoreCommonStandards.com

61
www.CoreCommonStandards.com

62
www.CoreCommonStandards.com

63
www.CoreCommonStandards.com

64
www.CoreCommonStandards.com

65
www.CoreCommonStandards.com

This is a Blank Page

You May Cut Out Resources On Back

This is a Blank Page

70
www.CoreCommonStandards.com

71
www.CoreCommonStandards.com

72
www.CoreCommonStandards.com

73
www.CoreCommonStandards.com

74
www.CoreCommonStandards.com

75
www.CoreCommonStandards.com

This is a Blank Page

You May Cut Out Resources On Back

This is a Blank Page

80
www.CoreCommonStandards.com

81
www.CoreCommonStandards.com

82
www.CoreCommonStandards.com

83
www.CoreCommonStandards.com

84
www.CoreCommonStandards.com

85
www.CoreCommonStandards.com

This is a Blank Page

You May Cut Out Resources On Back

This is a Blank Page

90
www.CoreCommonStandards.com

91
www.CoreCommonStandards.com

92
www.CoreCommonStandards.com

93
www.CoreCommonStandards.com

94
www.CoreCommonStandards.com

95
www.CoreCommonStandards.com

This is a Blank Page

You May Cut Out Resources On Back

This is a Blank Page

Name: _____

Adding Two-Digit Numbers

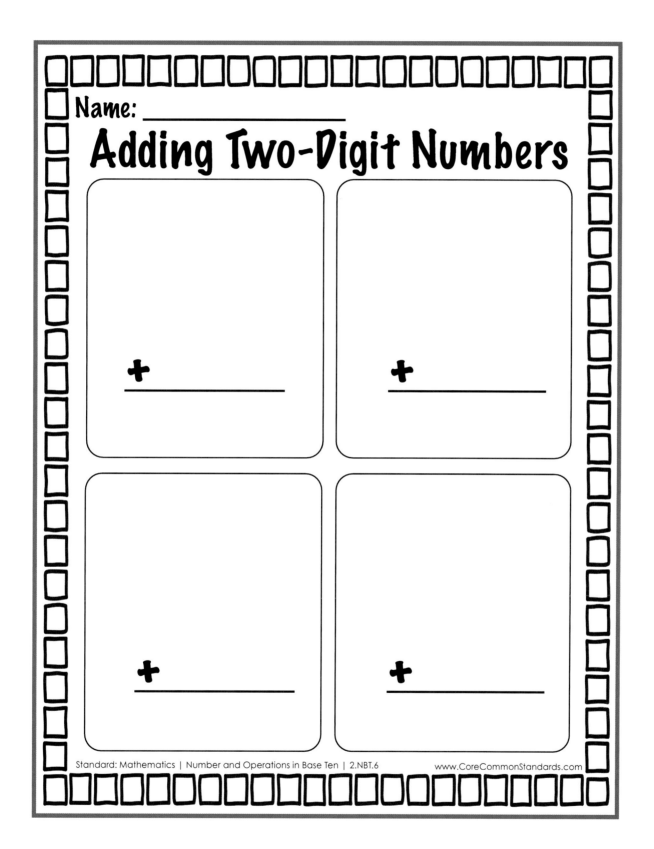

$+$ _____

$+$ _____

$+$ _____

$+$ _____

Standard: Mathematics | Number and Operations in Base Ten | 2.NBT.6   www.CoreCommonStandards.com

This is a Blank Page

You May Cut Out Resources On Back

This is a Blank Page

add & Subtract
With Frogs.

Directions:

Add and subtract within 1000, using concrete models or drawings and strategies based on place value, properties of operations, and/or the relationship between addition and subtraction; relate the strategy to a written method. Understand that in adding or subtracting three-digit numbers, one adds or subtracts hundreds and hundreds, tens and tens, ones and ones; and sometimes it is necessary to compose or decompose tens or hundreds.

Students shuffle cards and place them into equal piles. Students then flip over one card from each pile and use the spinner to determine if they will add or subtract the two numbers. Students will record answers in the activity sheet.

Standard: Math| Number and Operations in Base Ten| 2.NBT.7
Graphics by Scrappin Doodles   www.CoreCommonStandards.com

This is a Blank Page

You May Cut Out Resources On Back

This is a Blank Page

Subtract!

I need to borrow 1 from the hundred's column

$$
\begin{array}{r}
3\overset{1}{4}86 \\
-\ 191 \\
\hline
\ \ \ 5
\end{array}
$$

Standard: Math| Number and Operations in Base Ten| 2.NBT.7   www.CoreCommonStandards.com

This is a Blank Page

You May Cut Out Resources On Back

This is a Blank Page

Standard: Math| Number and Operations in Base Ten| 2.NBT.7   www.CoreCommonStandards.com

This is a Blank Page

You May Cut Out Resources On Back

This is a Blank Page

This is a Blank Page

You May Cut Out Resources On Back

This is a Blank Page

This is a Blank Page

You May Cut Out Resources On Back

This is a Blank Page

173

644

351

518

554

406

196

744

296

432

116

120

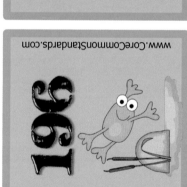

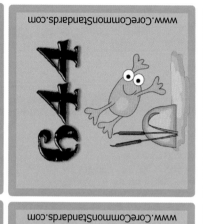

This is a Blank Page

You May Cut Out Resources On Back

This is a Blank Page

317

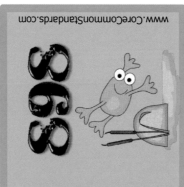

868

259

192

893

433

159

527

55

589

217

848

This is a Blank Page

You May Cut Out Resources On Back

This is a Blank Page

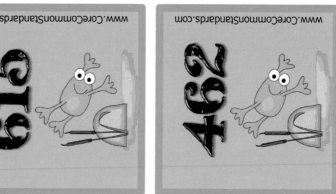

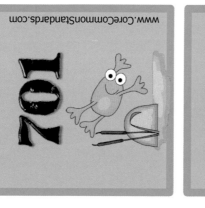

This is a Blank Page

You May Cut Out Resources On Back

This is a Blank Page

Number	Symbol	Number		Answer
500	+	100	=	600
			=	
			=	
			=	
			=	
			=	
			=	
			=	
			=	
			=	
			=	

Standard: Math| Number & Operations in Base Ten| 2.NBT.7   www.CoreCommonStandards.com

This is a Blank Page

You May Cut Out Resources On Back

This is a Blank Page

Popcorn
MENTAL MATH!

Cut out the popcorn cards and sort into two piles, red and blue.

For one minute, students flip one card per pile and answers the equation. Correct answers are placed in a separate pile.

After the minute, student records the correct equation and answer in the Popcorn Math Sheet!

Directions:

Mentally add 10 or 100 to a given number 100–900, and mentally subtract 10 or 100 from a given number 100–900.

Standard: Math| Number & Operations in Base Ten| 2.NBT.8
Graphics by Scrappin Doodles www.CoreCommonStandards.com

This is a Blank Page

You May Cut Out Resources On Back

This is a Blank Page

This is a Blank Page

You May Cut Out Resources On Back

This is a Blank Page

This is a Blank Page

You May Cut Out Resources On Back

This is a Blank Page

This is a Blank Page

You May Cut Out Resources On Back

This is a Blank Page

This is a Blank Page

You May Cut Out Resources On Back

This is a Blank Page

This is a Blank Page

You May Cut Out Resources On Back

This is a Blank Page

This is a Blank Page

You May Cut Out Resources On Back

This is a Blank Page

Number	Symbol	Number		Answer
500	+	100	=	600
			=	
			=	
			=	
			=	
			=	
			=	
			=	
			=	
			=	
			=	

Standard: Math| Number & Operations in Base Ten| 2.NBT.8   www.CoreCommonStandards.com

This is a Blank Page

You May Cut Out Resources On Back

This is a Blank Page

Why does it work?

Directions:

Explain why addition and subtraction strategies work, using place value and the properties of operations.

Students will create their own addition and subtraction problems, draw a picture, and explain why the strategies work.

4 + 6 = 10

Standard: Math| Number and Operations in Base Ten Standards| NBT.2.9   Images by clipart.com
www.CoreCommonStandards.com

This is a Blank Page

You May Cut Out Resources On Back

This is a Blank Page

Addition Problem

Picture:

+

=

Why does it work?

1+1=2
2+2=4
4+4=8

Standard: Math| Number and Operations in Base Ten Standards| NBT.2.9   www.CoreCommonStandards.com

This is a Blank Page

You May Cut Out Resources On Back

This is a Blank Page

Subtraction Problem

Picture:

Why does it work?

189

Standard: Math| Number and Operations in Base Ten Standards| NBT.2.9   www.CoreCommonStandards.com

This is a Blank Page

You May Cut Out Resources On Back

This is a Blank Page

Measure it!

Directions:
Measure the length of an object by selecting and using appropriate tools such as rulers, yardsticks, meter sticks, and measuring tapes.

Students practice measuring objects in a school with the appropriate tool.

Standard: Math| Measurement and Data| 2.MD.1
Graphics by Scrappin Doodles and clipart.com www.CoreCommonStandards.com

This is a Blank Page

You May Cut Out Resources On Back

This is a Blank Page

Name:_____

Measure it!

Object	Length	Tool Measured with

Standard: Math| Measurement and Data| 2.MD.1 www.CoreCommonStandards.com

This is a Blank Page

You May Cut Out Resources On Back

This is a Blank Page

How many inches is your pencil?

www.CoreCommonStandards.com

How many inches is your desk?

www.CoreCommonStandards.com

How many inches is your book?

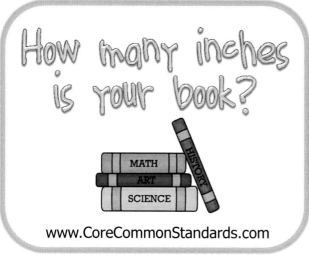

www.CoreCommonStandards.com

How many inches is your paper?

www.CoreCommonStandards.com

How many inches is the board?

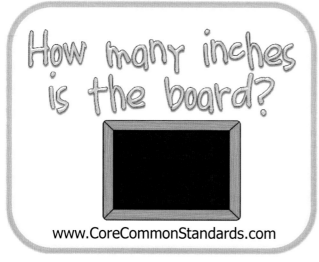

www.CoreCommonStandards.com

How many inches is a lunchbox?

www.CoreCommonStandards.com

This is a Blank Page

You May Cut Out Resources On Back

This is a Blank Page

How many inches
high is your chair?

www.CoreCommonStandards.com

How many inches
tall are you?

www.CoreCommonStandards.com

How many inches
tall is your
teacher?

www.CoreCommonStandards.com

How many inches
is your computer?

www.CoreCommonStandards.com

How many feet
is the school bus?

SCHOOL BUS

www.CoreCommonStandards.com

How many inches
is a backpack?

www.CoreCommonStandards.com

This is a Blank Page

You May Cut Out Resources On Back

This is a Blank Page

How many feet high is classroom?

www.CoreCommonStandards.com

How many inches are you from the door?

www.CoreCommonStandards.com

How many inches is your window?

www.CoreCommonStandards.com

How many inches is a flag?

www.CoreCommonStandards.com

How many inches is the bookcase?

www.CoreCommonStandards.com

How many inches is a television?

www.CoreCommonStandards.com

This is a Blank Page

You May Cut Out Resources On Back

This is a Blank Page

How many inches
is a paperclip?

How many inches
is a marker?

How many inches
is a eraser?

How many feet
is the gym?

How many inches
is a ruler?

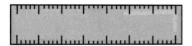

How many inches
is a crayon?

CRAYONS

This is a Blank Page

You May Cut Out Resources On Back

This is a Blank Page

Units of Measurement

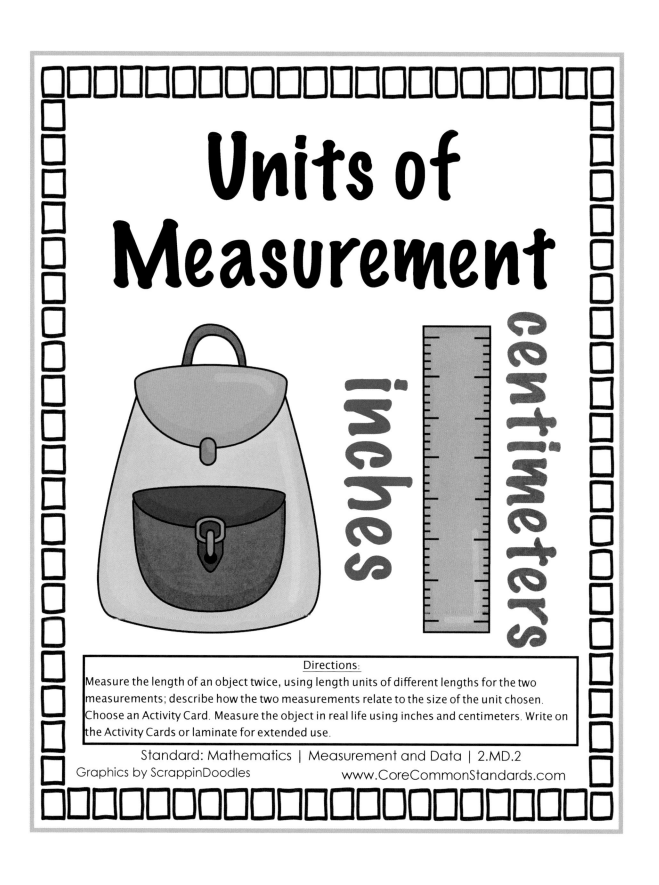

Directions:

Measure the length of an object twice, using length units of different lengths for the two measurements; describe how the two measurements relate to the size of the unit chosen. Choose an Activity Card. Measure the object in real life using inches and centimeters. Write on the Activity Cards or laminate for extended use.

Standard: Mathematics | Measurement and Data | 2.MD.2

Graphics by ScrappinDoodles

www.CoreCommonStandards.com

This is a Blank Page

You May Cut Out Resources On Back

This is a Blank Page

Backpack

Inches: _____

Centimeters: _____

Calculator

Inches: _____

Centimeters: _____

Crayon

Inches: _____

Centimeters: _____

Glue Bottle

Inches: _____

Centimeters: _____

This is a Blank Page

You May Cut Out Resources On Back

This is a Blank Page

Lunchbox

Inches: _____

Centimeters: _____

Paper

Inches: _____

Centimeters: _____

Pencil

Inches: _____

Centimeters: _____

Scissors

Inches: _____

Centimeters: _____

This is a Blank Page

You May Cut Out Resources On Back

This is a Blank Page

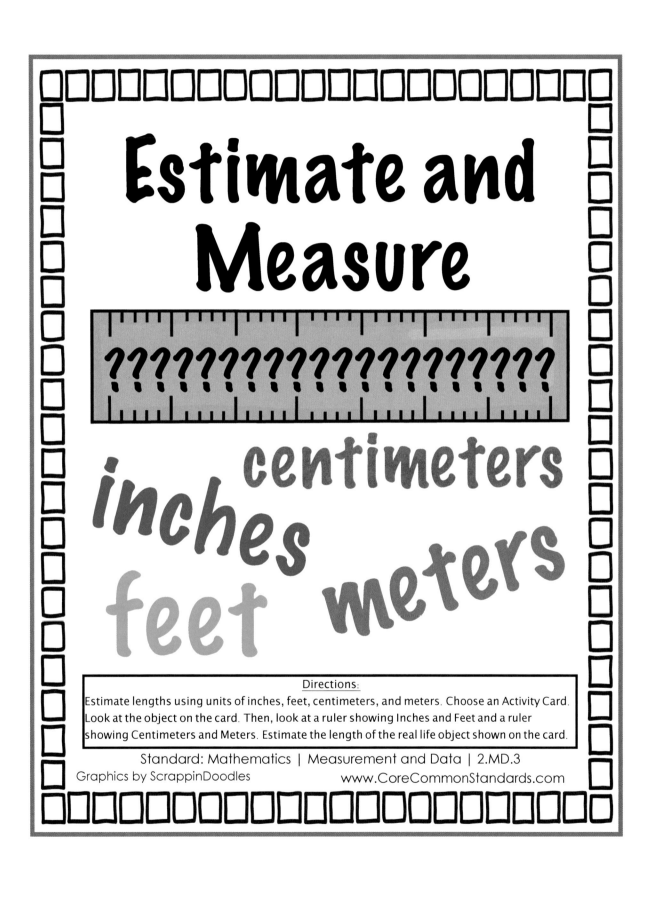

Estimate and Measure

?????????????????????????

centimeters

inches

feet meters

Directions:
Estimate lengths using units of inches, feet, centimeters, and meters. Choose an Activity Card. Look at the object on the card. Then, look at a ruler showing Inches and Feet and a ruler showing Centimeters and Meters. Estimate the length of the real life object shown on the card.

Standard: Mathematics | Measurement and Data | 2.MD.3

www.CoreCommonStandards.com

This is a Blank Page

You May Cut Out Resources On Back

This is a Blank Page

Backpack

Estimate the length of a backpack from top to bottom.

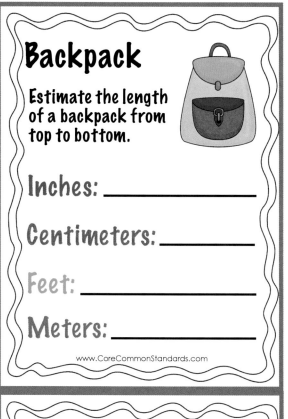

Inches: _____

Centimeters: _____

Feet: _____

Meters: _____

www.CoreCommonStandards.com

Calculator

Estimate the length of a calculator from top to bottom.

Inches: _____

Centimeters: _____

Feet: _____

Meters: _____

www.CoreCommonStandards.com

Crayon

Estimate the length of a crayon from top to bottom.

Inches: _____

Centimeters: _____

Feet: _____

Meters: _____

www.CoreCommonStandards.com

Glue Bottle

Estimate the length of a glue bottle from top to bottom.

Inches: _____

Centimeters: _____

Feet: _____

Meters: _____

www.CoreCommonStandards.com

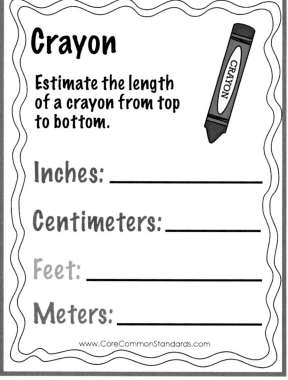

This is a Blank Page

You May Cut Out Resources On Back

This is a Blank Page

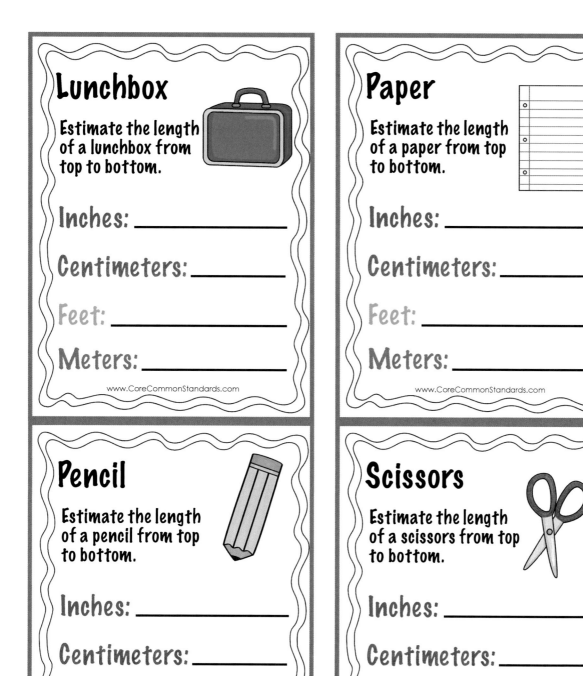

Lunchbox

Estimate the length of a lunchbox from top to bottom.

Inches: _____

Centimeters: _____

Feet: _____

Meters: _____

Paper

Estimate the length of a paper from top to bottom.

Inches: _____

Centimeters: _____

Feet: _____

Meters: _____

Pencil

Estimate the length of a pencil from top to bottom.

Inches: _____

Centimeters: _____

Feet: _____

Meters: _____

Scissors

Estimate the length of a scissors from top to bottom.

Inches: _____

Centimeters: _____

Feet: _____

Meters: _____

This is a Blank Page

You May Cut Out Resources On Back

This is a Blank Page

Dolphin

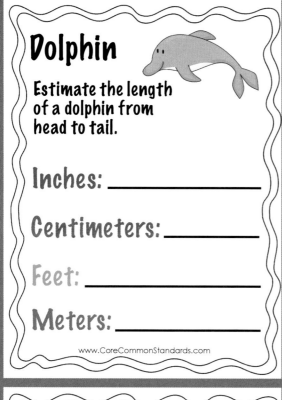

Estimate the length of a dolphin from head to tail.

Inches: _____

Centimeters: _____

Feet: _____

Meters: _____

Doghouse

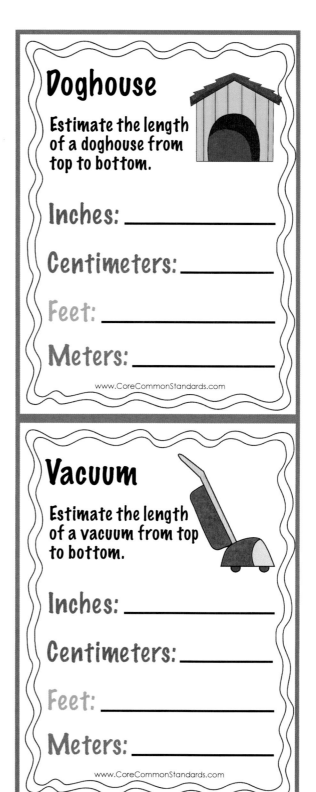

Estimate the length of a doghouse from top to bottom.

Inches: _____

Centimeters: _____

Feet: _____

Meters: _____

Computer

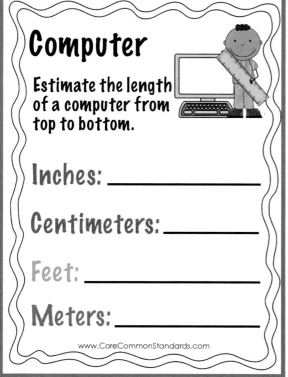

Estimate the length of a computer from top to bottom.

Inches: _____

Centimeters: _____

Feet: _____

Meters: _____

Vacuum

Estimate the length of a vacuum from top to bottom.

Inches: _____

Centimeters: _____

Feet: _____

Meters: _____

This is a Blank Page

You May Cut Out Resources On Back

This is a Blank Page

MEASURE IT!

Directions:

Measure to determine how much longer one object is than another, expressing the length difference in terms of a standard length unit.

Students practice measuring different objects in the classroom and then find the difference in length between the two objects.

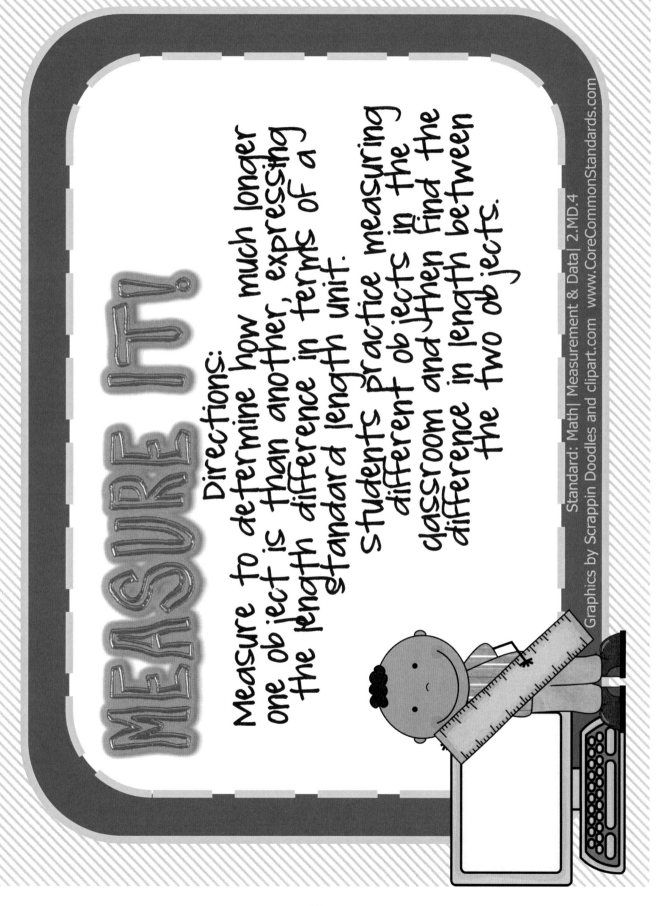

Standard: Math| Measurement & Data| 2.MD.4
Graphics by Scrappin Doodles and clipart.com   www.CoreCommonStandards.com

This is a Blank Page

You May Cut Out Resources On Back

This is a Blank Page

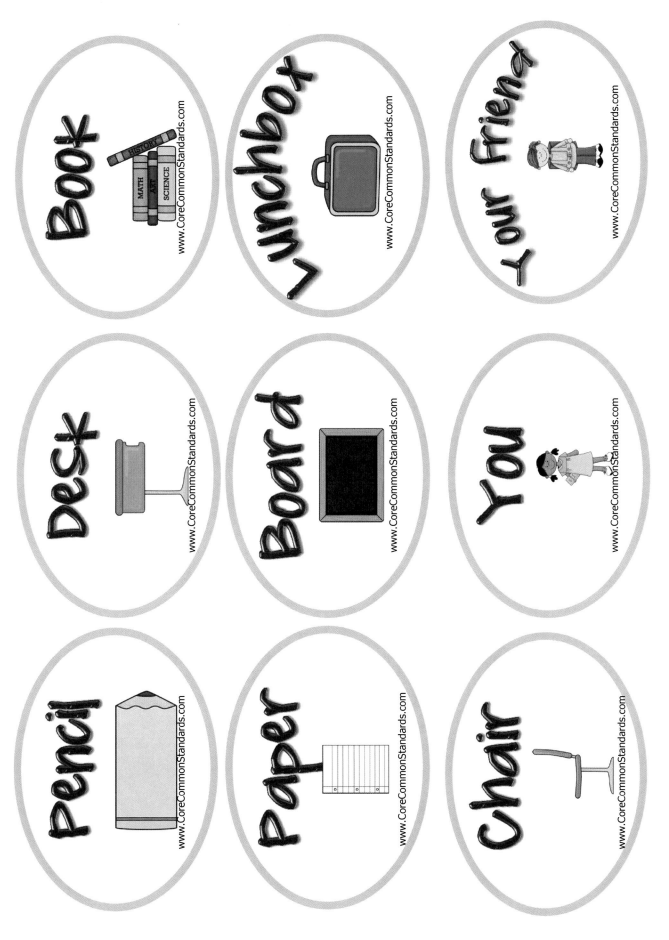

Book

www.CoreCommonStandards.com

Lunchbox

www.CoreCommonStandards.com

Your Friend

www.CoreCommonStandards.com

Desk

www.CoreCommonStandards.com

Board

www.CoreCommonStandards.com

You

www.CoreCommonStandards.com

Pencil

www.CoreCommonStandards.com

Paper

www.CoreCommonStandards.com

Chair

www.CoreCommonStandards.com

This is a Blank Page

You May Cut Out Resources On Back

This is a Blank Page

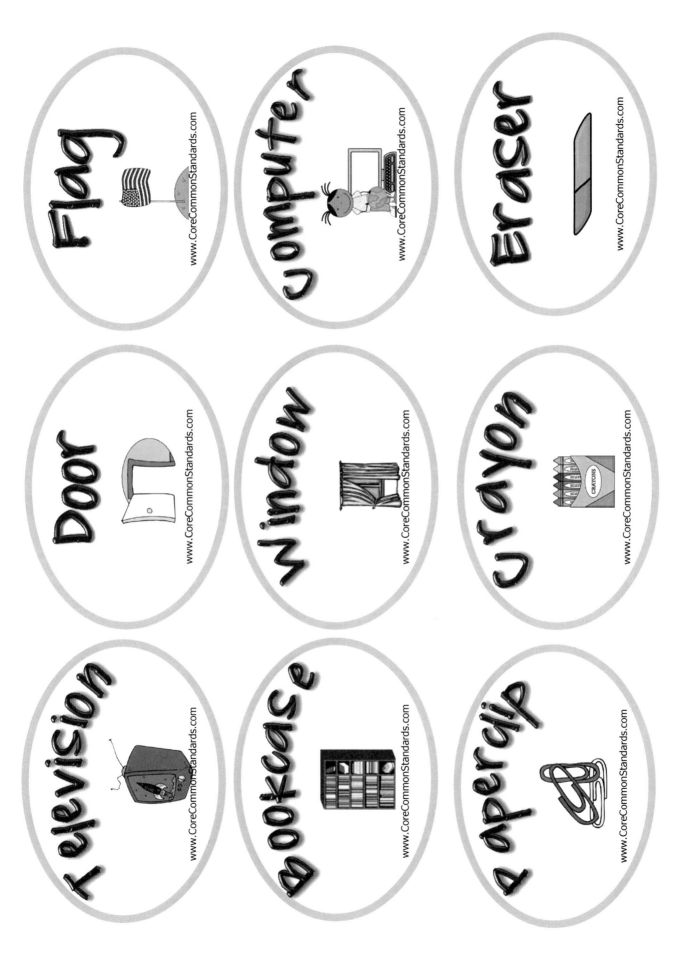

Flag

www.CoreCommonStandards.com

Computer

www.CoreCommonStandards.com

Eraser

www.CoreCommonStandards.com

Door

www.CoreCommonStandards.com

Window

www.CoreCommonStandards.com

Crayon

www.CoreCommonStandards.com

Television

www.CoreCommonStandards.com

Bookcase

www.CoreCommonStandards.com

Paperclip

www.CoreCommonStandards.com

This is a Blank Page

You May Cut Out Resources On Back

This is a Blank Page

Name: _____

object #1	Length	object #2	Length	Difference in lengths

www.CoreCommonStandards.com

Standard: Math| Measurement & Data| 2.MD.4

This is a Blank Page

You May Cut Out Resources On Back

This is a Blank Page

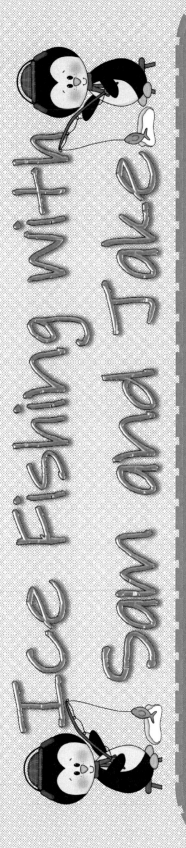

Ice Fishing with Sam and Jake

Use addition and subtraction within 100 to solve word problems involving lengths that are given in the same units, e.g., by using drawings (such as drawings of rulers) and equations with a symbol for the unknown number to represent the problem.

Students will solve addition and subtraction word problems using drawings and equations in their Measurement Math Journal! Extra pages are included for students to create their own math word problems.

Standard: Math| Measurement & Data| 2.MD.5
www.CoreCommonStandards.com

Graphics by Scrappin Doodles

This is a Blank Page

You May Cut Out Resources On Back

This is a Blank Page

Ice Fishing with Sam and Jake

Measurement Word Problems

Name:

Standard: Math | Measurement & Data | 2.MD.5

www.CoreCommonStandards.com

This is a Blank Page

You May Cut Out Resources On Back

This is a Blank Page

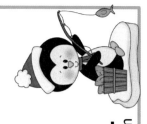

Sam caught a fish that was 5 inches long.
Jake caught a fish that was 6 inches longer.
How long was Jake's fish?

Draw it!

Equation:

◯ _____ = _____

Standard: Math| Measurement & Data| 2.MD.5   www.CoreCommonStandards.com

This is a Blank Page

You May Cut Out Resources On Back

This is a Blank Page

Sam's fishing line was 17 feet long. Jake's fishing line was 19 feet long. How long were they altogether ?

Draw it!

Equation: _____ ◯ _____ = _____

Standard: Math| Measurement & Data| 2.MD.5

This is a Blank Page

You May Cut Out Resources On Back

This is a Blank Page

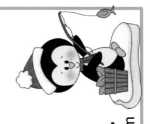

Sam's fishing hole was 22 feet deep. Jake's fishing hole was 29 feet deep. How much shorter is Sam's fishing hole than Jake's?

Draw it!

Equation: _____ ◯ _____ = _____

Standard: Math| Measurement & Data| 2.MD.5

www.CoreCommonStandards.com

This is a Blank Page

You May Cut Out Resources On Back

This is a Blank Page

Sam caught a fish that was 15 inches long.
Jake caught a fish that was 5 inches longer.
How long were their fish together?

Draw it!

Equation: _____ ◯ _____ = _____

Standard: Math| Measurement & Data| 2.MD.5

This is a Blank Page

You May Cut Out Resources On Back

This is a Blank Page

Sam's pile of fish was 31 inches high. Jake's pile of fish was 19 inches high. How many inches shorter is Jake's pile than Sam's?

Draw it!

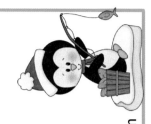

Equation: _____ ( ) = _____

Standard: Math| Measurement & Data| 2.MD.5

www.CoreCommonStandards.com

This is a Blank Page

You May Cut Out Resources On Back

This is a Blank Page

Sam and Jake went fishing on Saturday for 50 minutes. They went fishing on Sunday for 30 minutes. How many total minutes did they spend fishing that weekend?

Draw it!

Equation: _____ ◯ _____ = _____

Standard: Math| Measurement & Data| 2.MD.5   www.CoreCommonStandards.com

This is a Blank Page

You May Cut Out Resources On Back

This is a Blank Page

Let's use a number line!

Directions:

Represent whole numbers as lengths from 0 on a number line diagram with equally spaced points corresponding to the numbers 0, 1, 2, ..., and represent whole-number sums and differences within 100 on a number line diagram.

Students will shuffle cards and place in a pile. Students will begin at fifty on the number line and then move based on the directions on the card. As students move on the number line, they will write the equation on the score sheet. The first player to 100 wins!

Laminate number lines and score sheets for multiple uses!

Standard: Math| Measurement & Data| 2.MD.6
www.CoreCommonStandards.com

Graphics by Scrappin Doodles

This is a Blank Page

You May Cut Out Resources On Back

This is a Blank Page

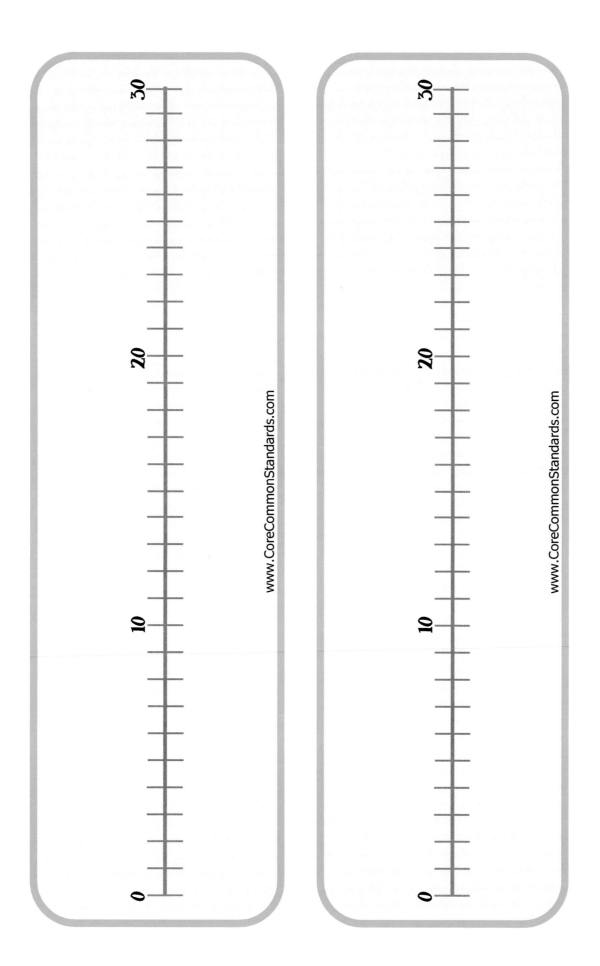

This is a Blank Page

You May Cut Out Resources On Back

This is a Blank Page

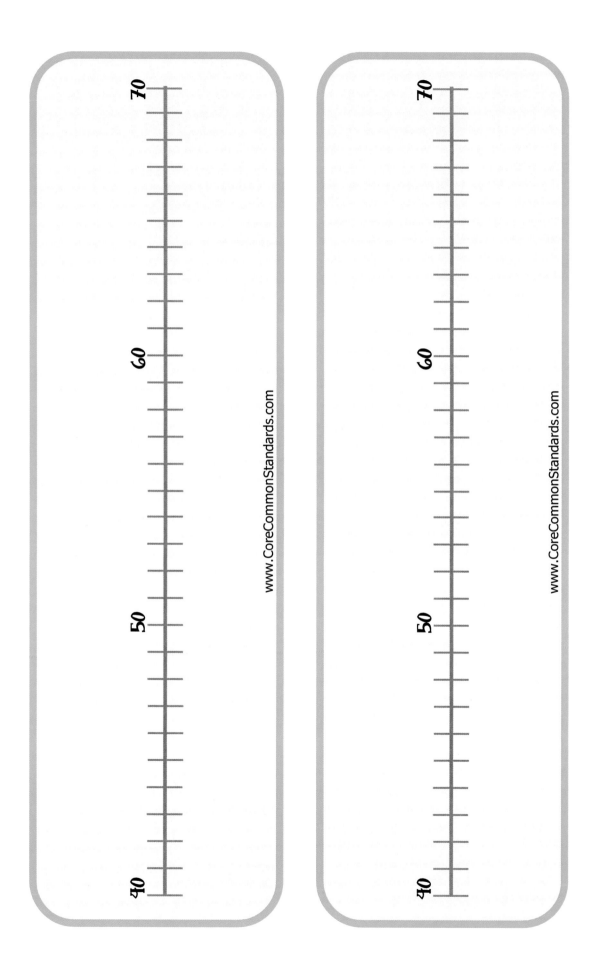

This is a Blank Page

You May Cut Out Resources On Back

This is a Blank Page

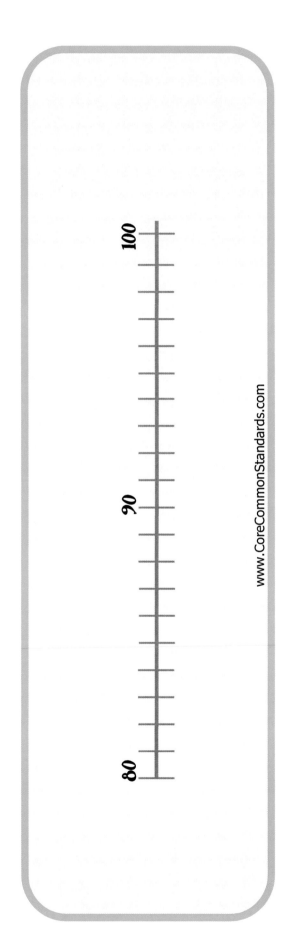

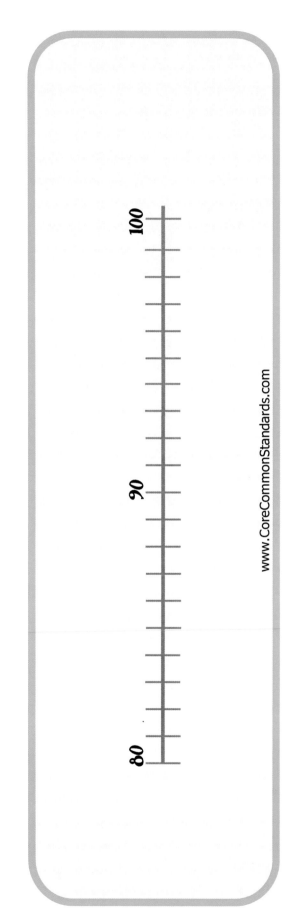

This is a Blank Page

You May Cut Out Resources On Back

This is a Blank Page

Jump
forward
2

Jump
forward
5

Jump
forward
9

Jump
forward
7

Jump
forward
1

Jump
forward
8

Jump
forward
3

Jump
forward
10

Jump
forward
6

This is a Blank Page

You May Cut Out Resources On Back

This is a Blank Page

Jump forward 2
www.CoreCommonStandards.com

Jump forward 5
www.CoreCommonStandards.com

Jump forward 9
www.CoreCommonStandards.com

Jump forward 7
www.CoreCommonStandards.com

Jump forward 1
www.CoreCommonStandards.com

Jump forward 8
www.CoreCommonStandards.com

Jump forward 3
www.CoreCommonStandards.com

Jump forward 10
www.CoreCommonStandards.com

Jump forward 6
www.CoreCommonStandards.com

This is a Blank Page

You May Cut Out Resources On Back

This is a Blank Page

Jump
forward
2
www.CoreCommonStandards.com

Jump
forward
5
www.CoreCommonStandards.com

Jump
forward
9
www.CoreCommonStandards.com

Jump
forward
7
www.CoreCommonStandards.com

Jump
forward
1
www.CoreCommonStandards.com

Jump
forward
8
www.CoreCommonStandards.com

Jump
forward
3
www.CoreCommonStandards.com

Jump
forward
10
www.CoreCommonStandards.com

Jump
forward
6
www.CoreCommonStandards.com

This is a Blank Page

You May Cut Out Resources On Back

This is a Blank Page

Jump forward 2

www.CoreCommonStandards.com

Jump forward 5

www.CoreCommonStandards.com

Jump forward 9

www.CoreCommonStandards.com

Jump forward 7

www.CoreCommonStandards.com

Jump forward 1

www.CoreCommonStandards.com

Jump forward 8

www.CoreCommonStandards.com

Jump forward 3

www.CoreCommonStandards.com

Jump forward 10

www.CoreCommonStandards.com

Jump forward 6

www.CoreCommonStandards.com

This is a Blank Page

You May Cut Out Resources On Back

This is a Blank Page

Jump back 2

Jump back 5

Jump back 9

Jump back 7

Jump back 1

Jump back 8

Jump back 3

Jump back 10

Jump back 6

This is a Blank Page

You May Cut Out Resources On Back

This is a Blank Page

Jump back
2
www.CoreCommonStandards.com

Jump back
5
www.CoreCommonStandards.com

Jump back
9
www.CoreCommonStandards.com

Jump back
7
www.CoreCommonStandards.com

Jump back
1
www.CoreCommonStandards.com

Jump back
8
www.CoreCommonStandards.com

Jump back
3
www.CoreCommonStandards.com

Jump back
10
www.CoreCommonStandards.com

Jump back
6
www.CoreCommonStandards.com

This is a Blank Page

You May Cut Out Resources On Back

This is a Blank Page

Number	Symbol	Number		Solution
50			=	
			=	
			=	
			=	
			=	
			=	
			=	
			=	
			=	
			=	
			=	
			=	
			=	
			=	

Standard: Math| Measurement & Data| 2.MD.6

www.CoreCommonStandards.com

This is a Blank Page

You May Cut Out Resources On Back

This is a Blank Page

WHAT TIME IS IT?!

Directions:

Tell and write time from analog and digital clocks to the nearest five minutes, using a.m. and p.m.

Label a clock to review before playing dominoes to match analog and digital clocks to their numerical time.

Then, students can continue to practice telling and writing time using analog clocks.

Standard: Math| Measurement and Data| 2.MD.7

Graphics by Scrappin Doodles and clipart.com   www.CoreCommonStandards.com

This is a Blank Page

You May Cut Out Resources On Back

This is a Blank Page

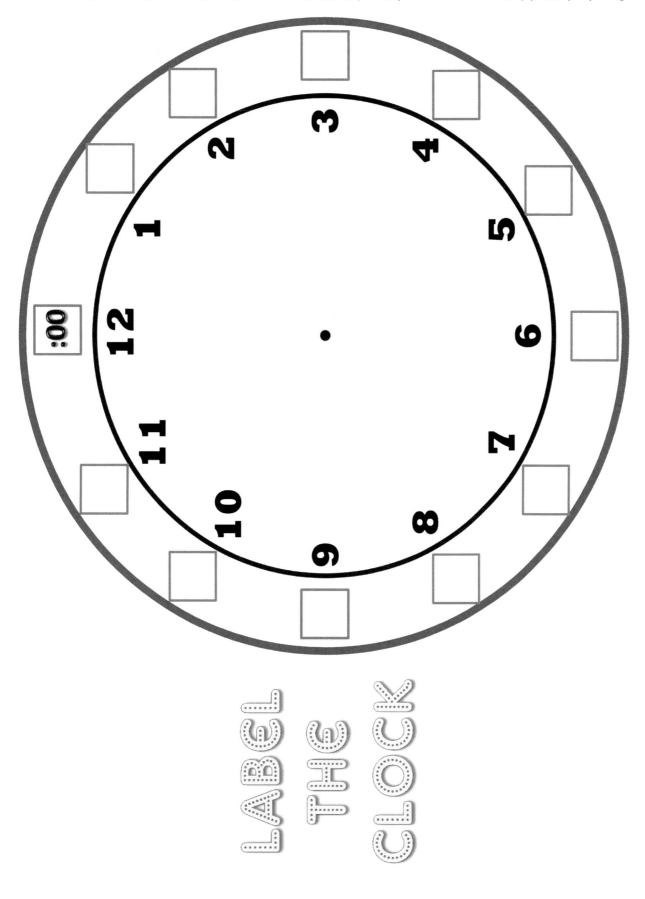

LABEL THE CLOCK

This is a Blank Page

You May Cut Out Resources On Back

This is a Blank Page

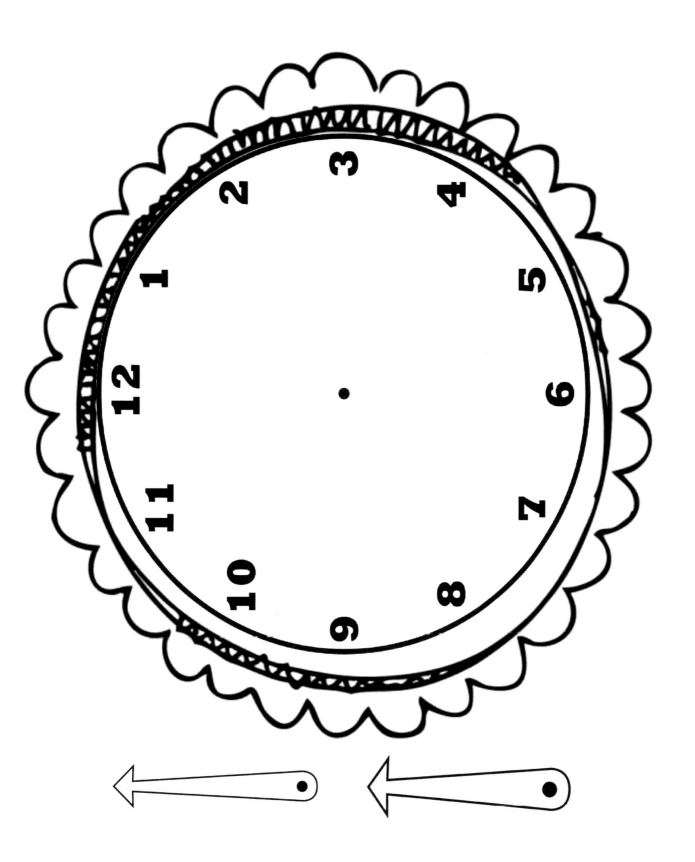

This is a Blank Page

You May Cut Out Resources On Back

This is a Blank Page

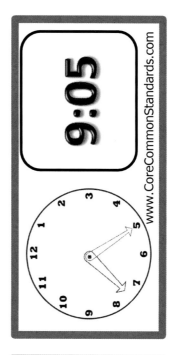

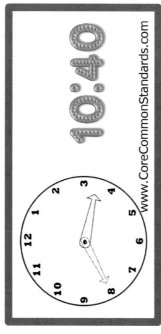

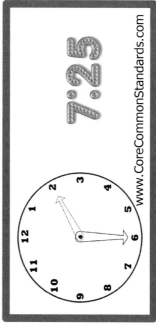

This is a Blank Page

You May Cut Out Resources On Back

This is a Blank Page

1:00

1:00   12:50

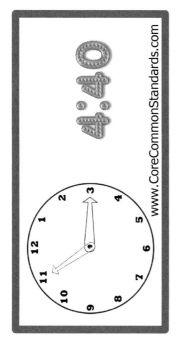

4:40

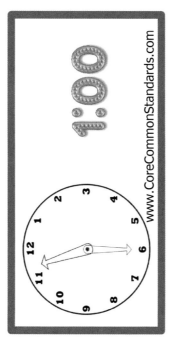

1:00

8:50

3:25

2:55

8:55

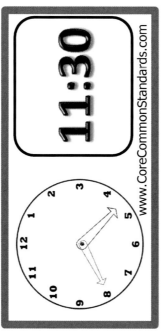

11:30

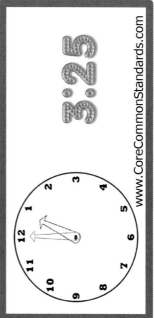

3:25

This is a Blank Page

You May Cut Out Resources On Back

This is a Blank Page

6:20

6:20   3:00

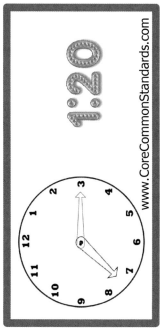

1:20

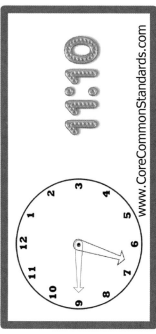

11:10

7:05

2:45

7:15

12:50

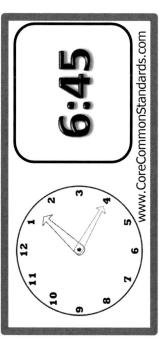

6:45

2:45

This is a Blank Page

You May Cut Out Resources On Back

This is a Blank Page

Name:_____

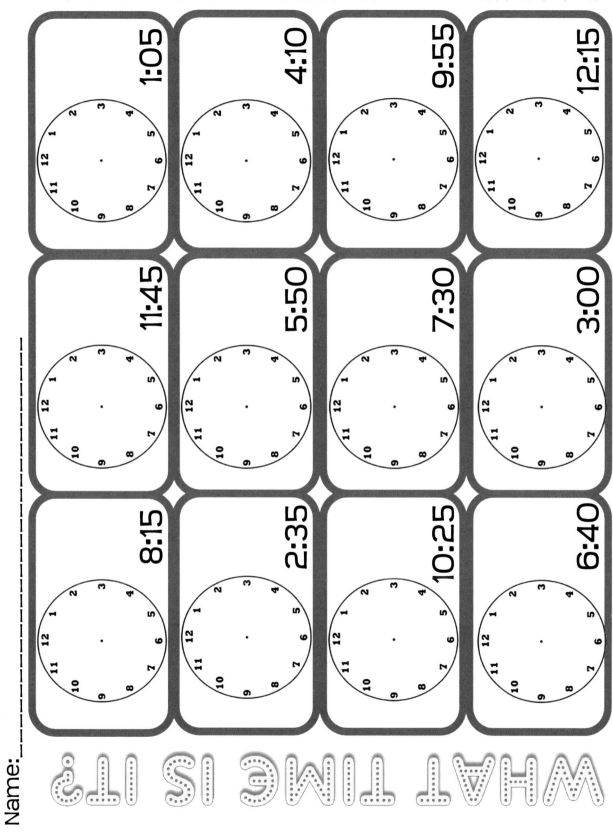

WHAT TIME IS IT?

1:05	4:10	9:55	12:15
11:45	5:50	7:30	3:00
8:15	2:35	10:25	6:40

This is a Blank Page

You May Cut Out Resources On Back

This is a Blank Page

Name: _____

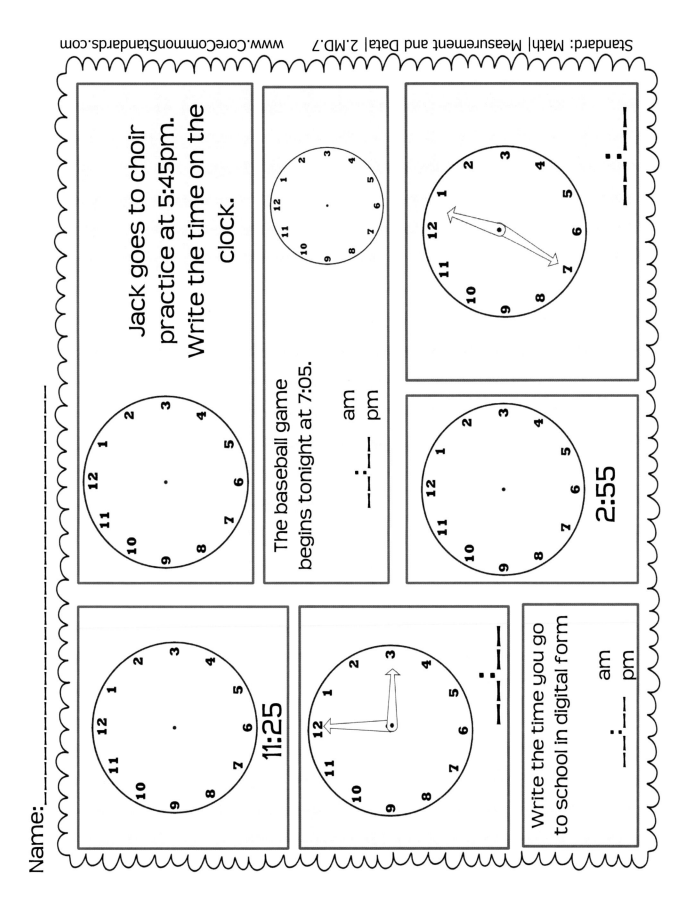

Jack goes to choir practice at 5:45pm. Write the time on the clock.

The baseball game begins tonight at 7:05.

_ _ : _ _

○ am
○ pm

2:55

11:25

Write the time you go to school in digital form

_ _ : _ _

○ am
○ pm

This is a Blank Page

You May Cut Out Resources On Back

This is a Blank Page

Let's go Shopping!

Directions:

Solve word problems involving dollar bills, quarters, dimes, nickels, and pennies, using $ and ¢ symbols appropriately. Example: If you have 2 dimes and 3 pennies, how many cents do you have?

Review money amounts before you go shopping to make sure that you don't pay too much or too little for your items!

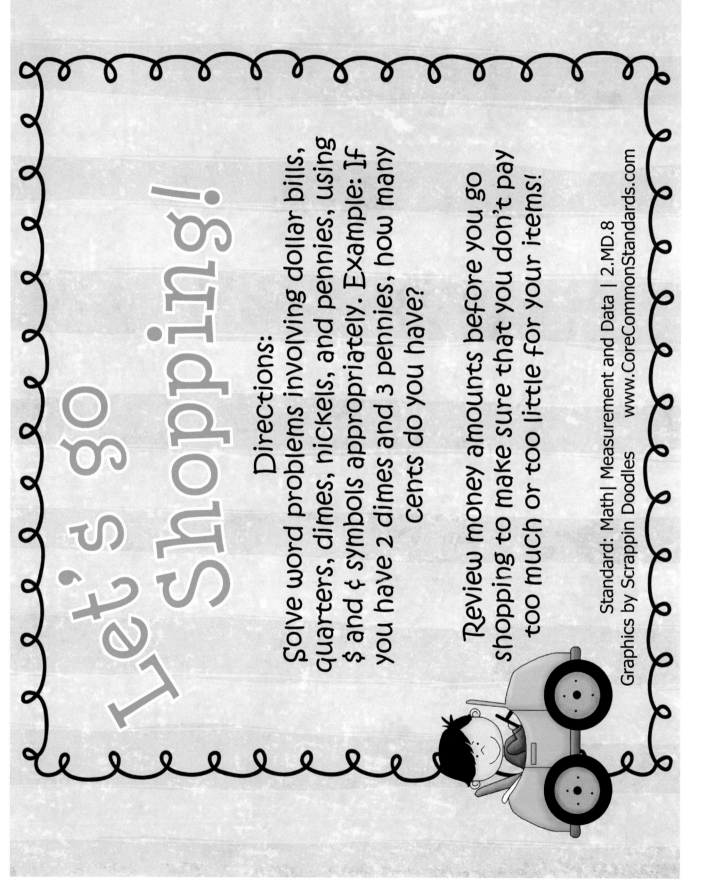

Standard: Math| Measurement and Data | 2.MD.8
Graphics by Scrappin Doodles   www.CoreCommonStandards.com

This is a Blank Page

You May Cut Out Resources On Back

This is a Blank Page

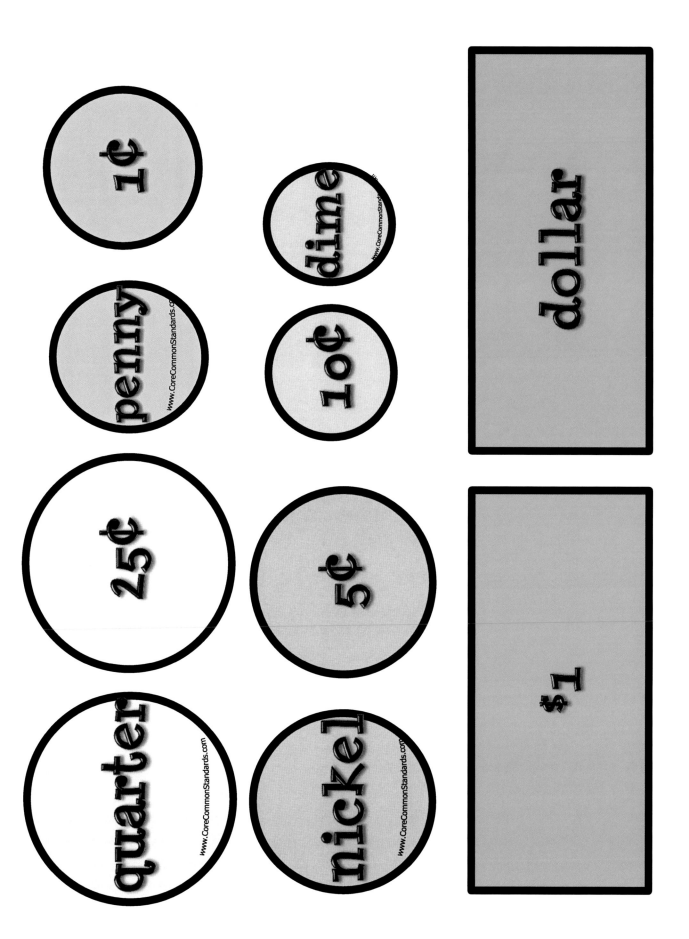

This is a Blank Page

You May Cut Out Resources On Back

This is a Blank Page

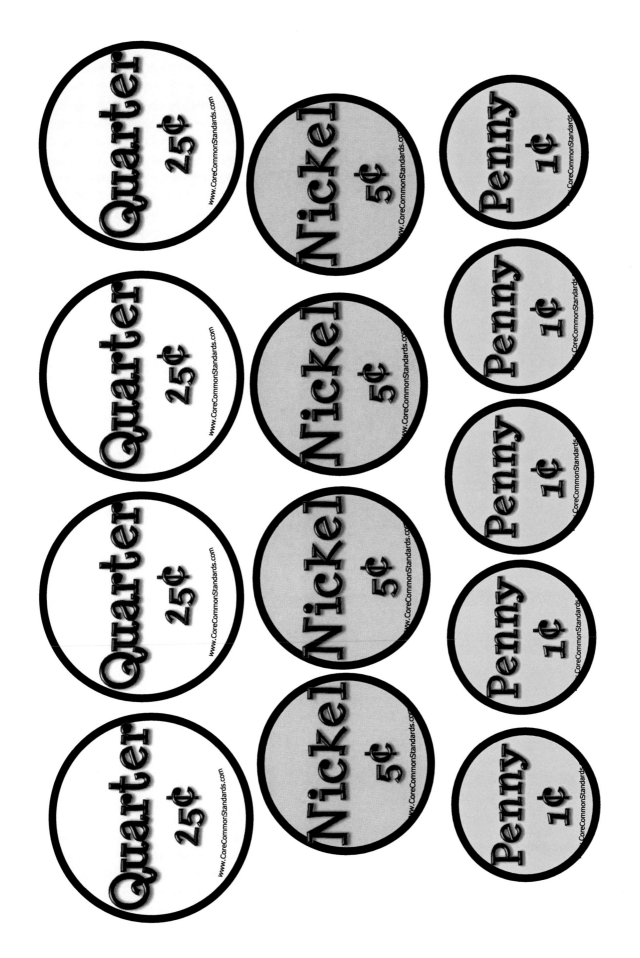

283

This is a Blank Page

You May Cut Out Resources On Back

This is a Blank Page

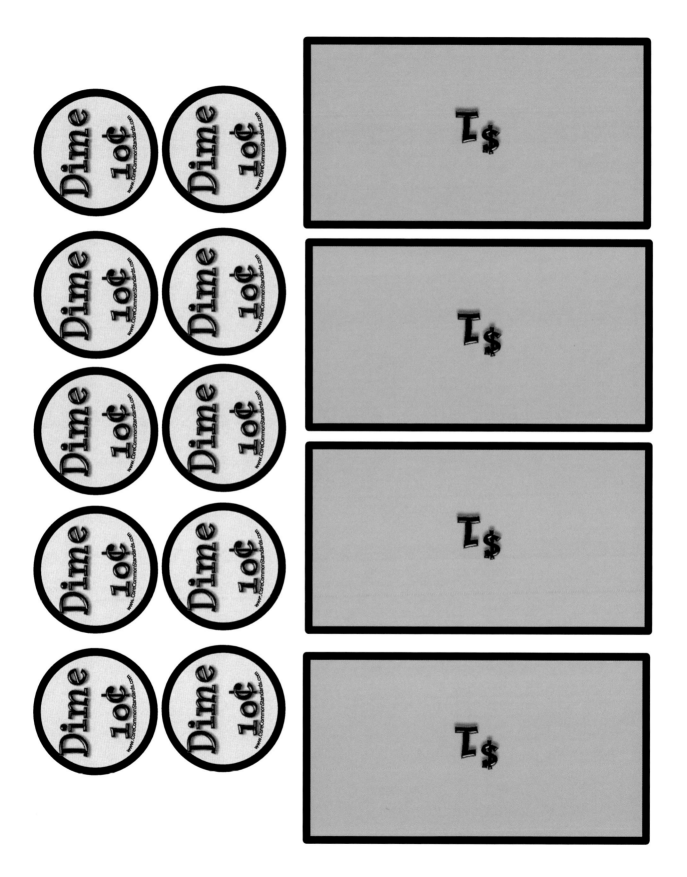

This is a Blank Page

You May Cut Out Resources On Back

This is a Blank Page

How much!?

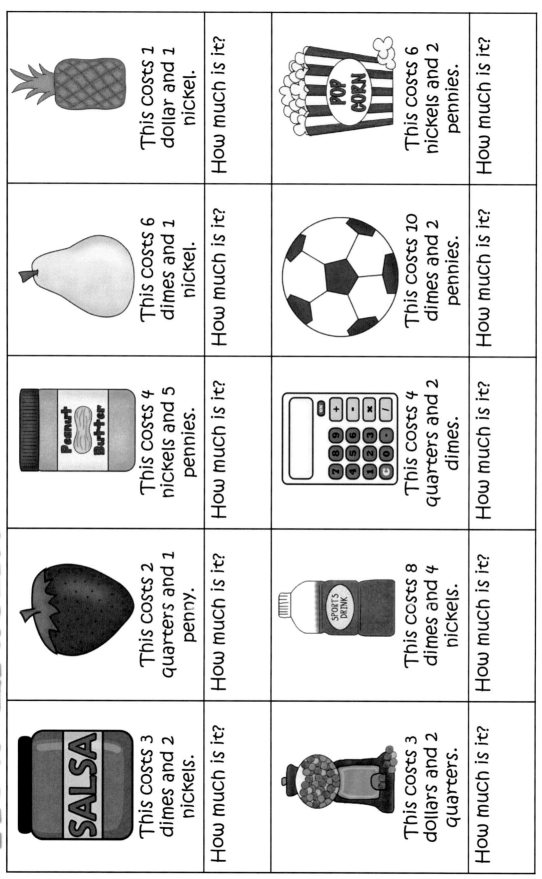

This costs 3 dimes and 2 nickels.	This costs 2 quarters and 1 penny.	This costs 4 nickels and 5 pennies.	This costs 6 dimes and 1 nickel.	This costs 1 dollar and 1 nickel.
How much is it?	How much is it?	How much is it?	How much is it?	How much is it?
This costs 3 dollars and 2 quarters.	This costs 8 dimes and 4 nickels.	This costs 4 quarters and 2 dimes.	This costs 10 dimes and 2 pennies.	This costs 6 nickels and 2 pennies.
How much is it?	How much is it?	How much is it?	How much is it?	How much is it?

Standard: Math| Measure and Data | 2.MD.8   www.CoreCommonStandards.com

This is a Blank Page

You May Cut Out Resources On Back

This is a Blank Page

Measure and Plot

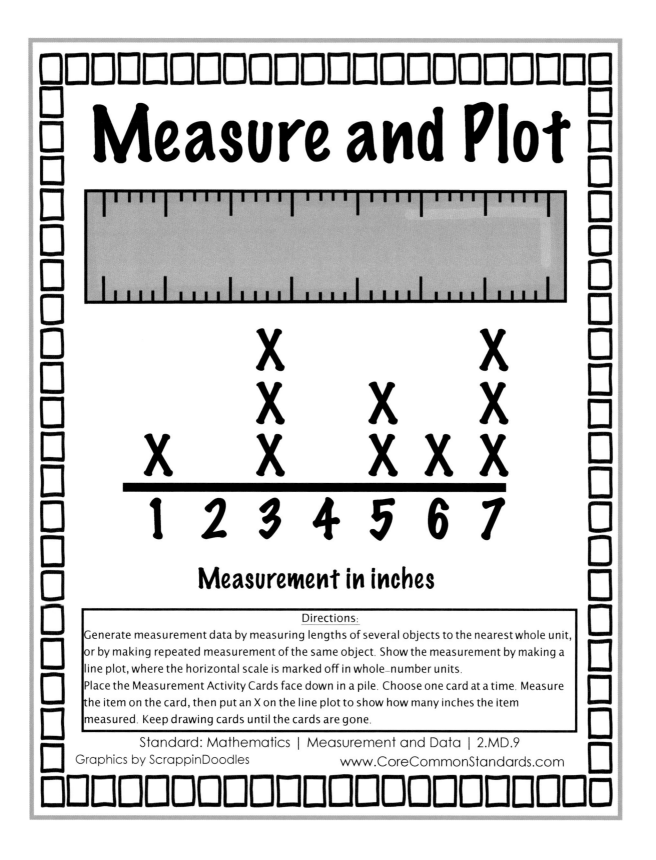

Measurement in inches

Directions:
Generate measurement data by measuring lengths of several objects to the nearest whole unit, or by making repeated measurement of the same object. Show the measurement by making a line plot, where the horizontal scale is marked off in whole-number units.
Place the Measurement Activity Cards face down in a pile. Choose one card at a time. Measure the item on the card, then put an X on the line plot to show how many inches the item measured. Keep drawing cards until the cards are gone.

Standard: Mathematics | Measurement and Data | 2.MD.9
Graphics by ScrappinDoodles
www.CoreCommonStandards.com

This is a Blank Page

You May Cut Out Resources On Back

This is a Blank Page

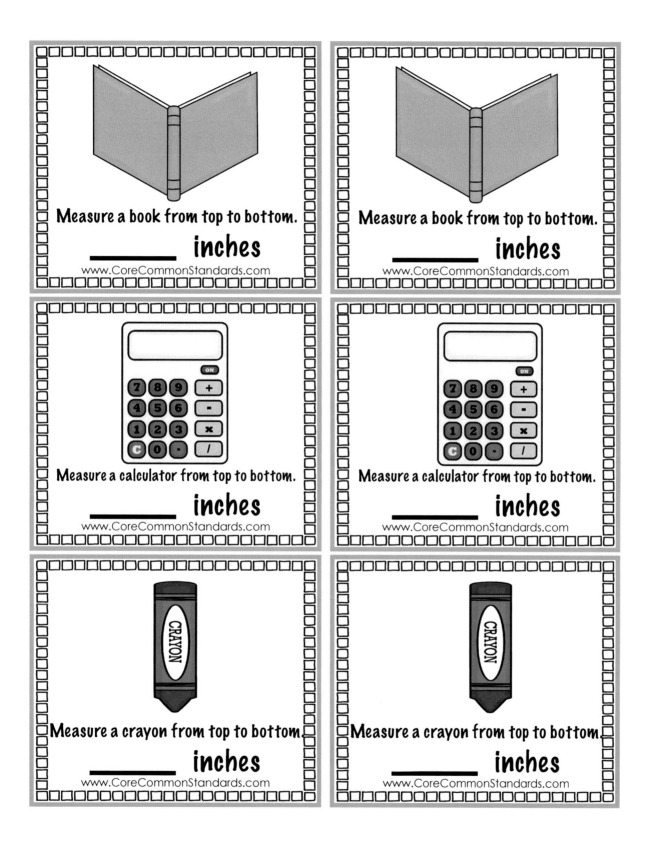

Measure a book from top to bottom.

_____ inches

www.CoreCommonStandards.com

Measure a book from top to bottom.

_____ inches

www.CoreCommonStandards.com

Measure a calculator from top to bottom.

_____ inches

www.CoreCommonStandards.com

Measure a calculator from top to bottom.

_____ inches

www.CoreCommonStandards.com

Measure a crayon from top to bottom.

_____ inches

www.CoreCommonStandards.com

Measure a crayon from top to bottom.

_____ inches

www.CoreCommonStandards.com

This is a Blank Page

You May Cut Out Resources On Back

This is a Blank Page

Measure a crayon box from top to bottom.

_____ inches

www.CoreCommonStandards.com

Measure a crayon box from top to bottom.

_____ inches

www.CoreCommonStandards.com

Measure a glue bottle from top to bottom.

_____ inches

www.CoreCommonStandards.com

Measure a glue bottle from top to bottom.

_____ inches

www.CoreCommonStandards.com

Measure a lunchbox from top to bottom.

_____ inches

www.CoreCommonStandards.com

Measure a lunchbox from top to bottom.

_____ inches

www.CoreCommonStandards.com

This is a Blank Page

You May Cut Out Resources On Back

This is a Blank Page

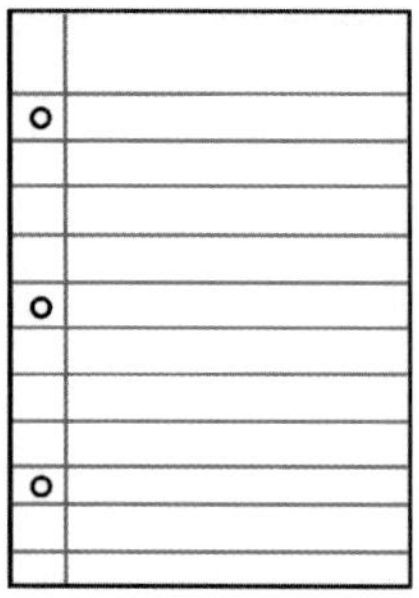

Measure a piece of paper from top to bottom.

_______ **inches**

www.CoreCommonStandards.com

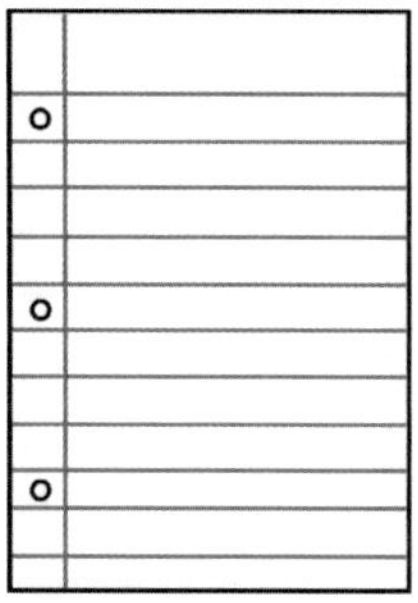

Measure a piece of paper from top to bottom.

_______ **inches**

www.CoreCommonStandards.com

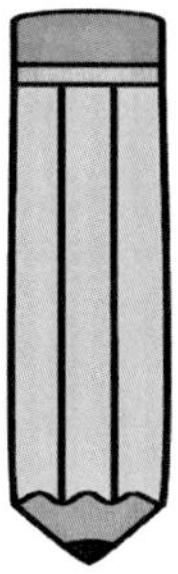

Measure a pencil from top to bottom.

_______ **inches**

www.CoreCommonStandards.com

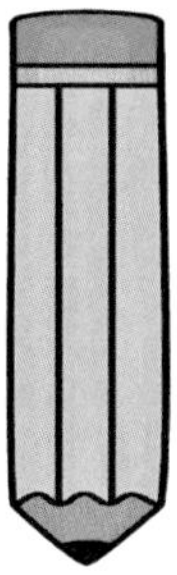

Measure a pencil from top to bottom.

_______ **inches**

www.CoreCommonStandards.com

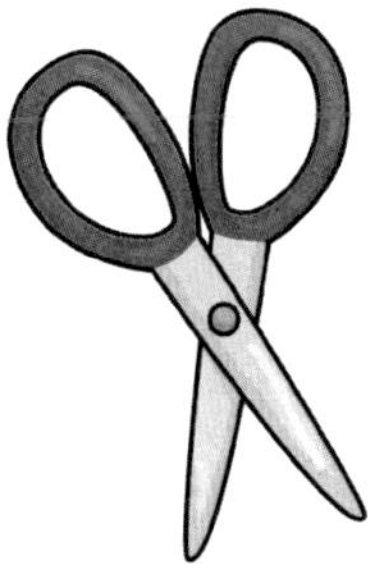

Measure scissors from top to bottom.

_______ **inches**

www.CoreCommonStandards.com

Measure scissors from top to bottom.

_______ **inches**

www.CoreCommonStandards.com

This is a Blank Page

You May Cut Out Resources On Back

This is a Blank Page

Name: _____

Directions: Draw a card, measure the item in inches, then put an X above that number on the line plot below.

Measure and Plot

1 2 3 4 5 6 7 8 9 10 11 12

Measurement in inches

This is a Blank Page

You May Cut Out Resources On Back

This is a Blank Page

Let's Make a Bar Graph!

Directions:

Draw a picture graph and a bar graph (with single-unit scale) to represent a data set with up to four categories. Solve simple put-together, take-apart, and compare problems using information presented in a bar graph.

Students survey classmates to find out their favorite fruits. Then, they create a bar graph to display their data and answer questions.

Standard: Math| Measurement and Data| 2.MD.10
Clipart by Scrappin' Doodles www.CoreCommonStandards.com

This is a Blank Page

You May Cut Out Resources On Back

This is a Blank Page

Find out your classmates favorite fruit & color the picture graph.

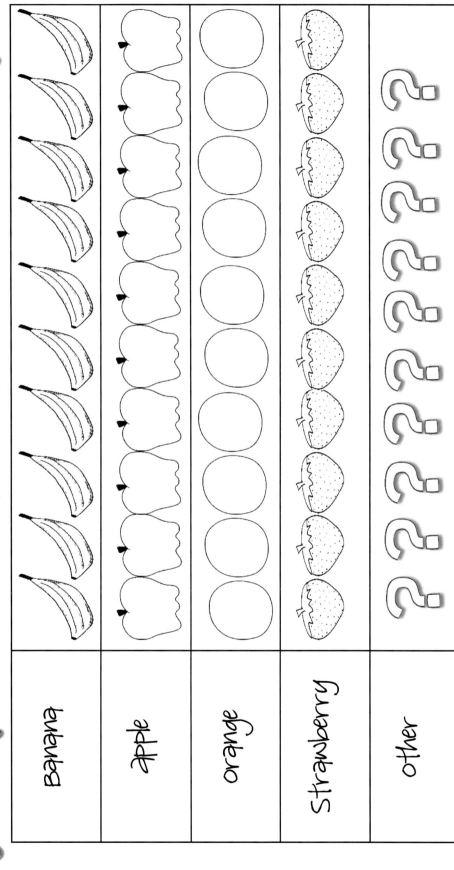

Banana										
apple										
orange										
Strawberry										
other										

Standard: Math| Measurement and Data| 2.MD.10

ww.CoreCommonStandards.com

This is a Blank Page

You May Cut Out Resources On Back

This is a Blank Page

Which fruit is your favorite?

10					
9					
8					
7					
6					
5					
4					
3					
2					
1					
	Banana	Apple	Orange	Strawberry	Other

1) Which fruit is the favorite?
_____

2) Which fruit is the least favorite?
_____

3) What is the difference between the number of students who like apples and bananas?
_____

4) How many students participated in the survey?
_____

5) If four more students liked oranges, how many students would have chosen oranges?
_____

6) What is a type of fruit that could be in the other category?
_____

7) How many students like a red fruit? _____

Standard: Math| Measurement and Data| 2.MD.10

This is a Blank Page

You May Cut Out Resources On Back

This is a Blank Page

MAGIC SHAPES

Directions:

Recognize and draw shapes having specified attributes, such as a given number of angles or a given number of equal faces. Identify triangles, quadrilaterals, pentagons, hexagons, and cubes.

Use the Shape Activity Cards to give clues to your partner. Read one clue at a time while your partner guesses the shape that is on the card. If your partner can guess the shape after Clue #1, they get 4 points. If they guess the shape after Clue #2, they get 3 points, and so on.

Players move the amount of spaces on the game board. First player to the end wins!

Standard: Math| Geometry| 2.G.1   www.CoreCommonStandards.com

Graphics by Scrappin Doodles and clipart.com

This is a Blank Page

You May Cut Out Resources On Back

This is a Blank Page

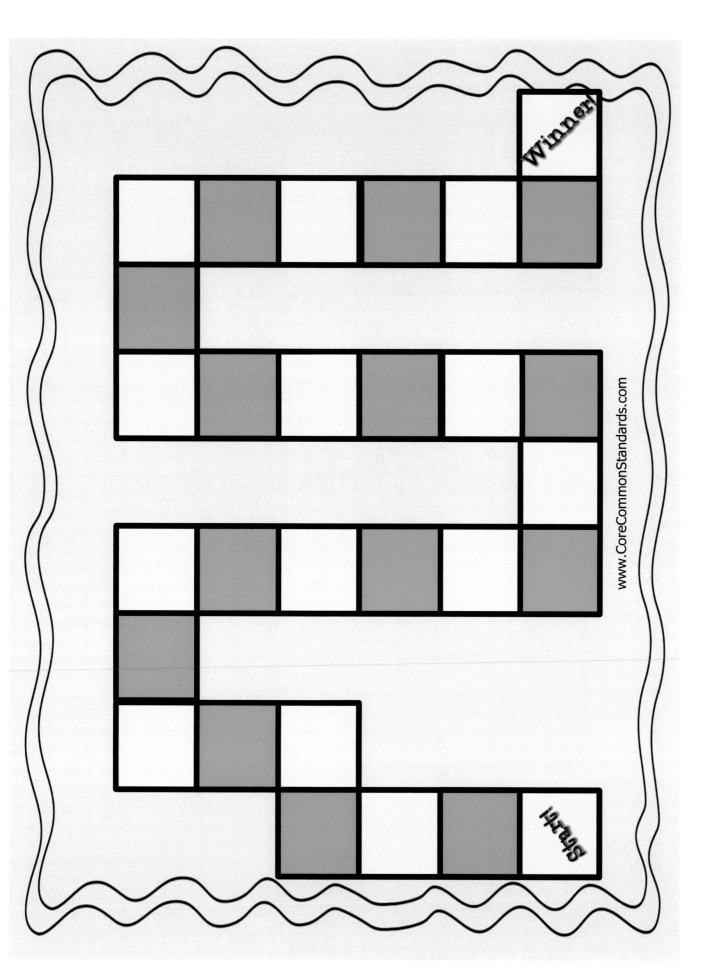

Winner!

Start!

This is a Blank Page

You May Cut Out Resources On Back

This is a Blank Page

Triangle

Clue #1: It's a 2-d Shape (4)

Clue #2: Sandwiches can be cut in this shape. (3)

Clue #3: This shape has 3 angles (2)

Clue #4: It has 3 sides (1)

www.CoreCommonStandards.com

Hexagon

Clue #1: It's a 2-d Shape (4)

Clue #2: A stop sign is this shape. (3)

Clue #3: This shape has 6 angle. (2)

Clue #4: This shape has 6 sides. (1)

www.CoreCommonStandards.com

Square

Clue #1: It's a 2-d Shape (4)

Clue #2: It has 4 sides (3)

Clue #3: All sides are equal in length (2)

Clue #4: It has 4 right angles (1)

www.CoreCommonStandards.com

Pentagon

Clue #1: It's a 2-d Shape (4)

Clue #2: Home plate at a baseball stadium is this shape. (3)

Clue #3: This shape has 5 angles. (2)

Clue #4: This shape has 5 sides. (1)

www.CoreCommonStandards.com

This is a Blank Page

You May Cut Out Resources On Back

This is a Blank Page

Trapezoid

Clue #1: It's a 2-d Shape (4)
Clue #2: It has 4 sides (3)
Clue #3: The parallel sides are bases (2)
Clue #4 One pair of parallel sides (1)

Cube

Clue #1: It's a 3-d Shape(4)
Clue #2: It has 12 edges (3)
Clue #3: It has 6 faces (2)
Clue #4: Each face is a square (1)

Rectangle

Clue #1: It's a 2-d Shape (4)
Clue #2: It has 4 sides (3)
Clue #3: It has 4 right angles (2)
Clue #4: All sides aren't equal in length (1)

Rhombus

Clue #1: It's a 2D shape (4)
Clue #2: It looks like a diamond (3)
Clue #3: The opposite sides are parallel (2)
Clue #4: All sides are equal in length (1)

This is a Blank Page

You May Cut Out Resources On Back

This is a Blank Page

Sharing chocolate!

Directions:

Partition a rectangle into rows and columns of same-size squares and count to find the total number of them.

Students will roll the die and then split the chocolate bar into that number of equal pieces. For additional practice, students can start with one die and then, use two dice. After the activity, students can use the activity page to continue practicing!

Laminate chocolate bar mat for and use dry erase markers for extended use.

Standard: Math| Geometry| 2.G.2   www.CoreCommonStandards.com

Graphics by Scrappin Doodles

This is a Blank Page

You May Cut Out Resources On Back

This is a Blank Page

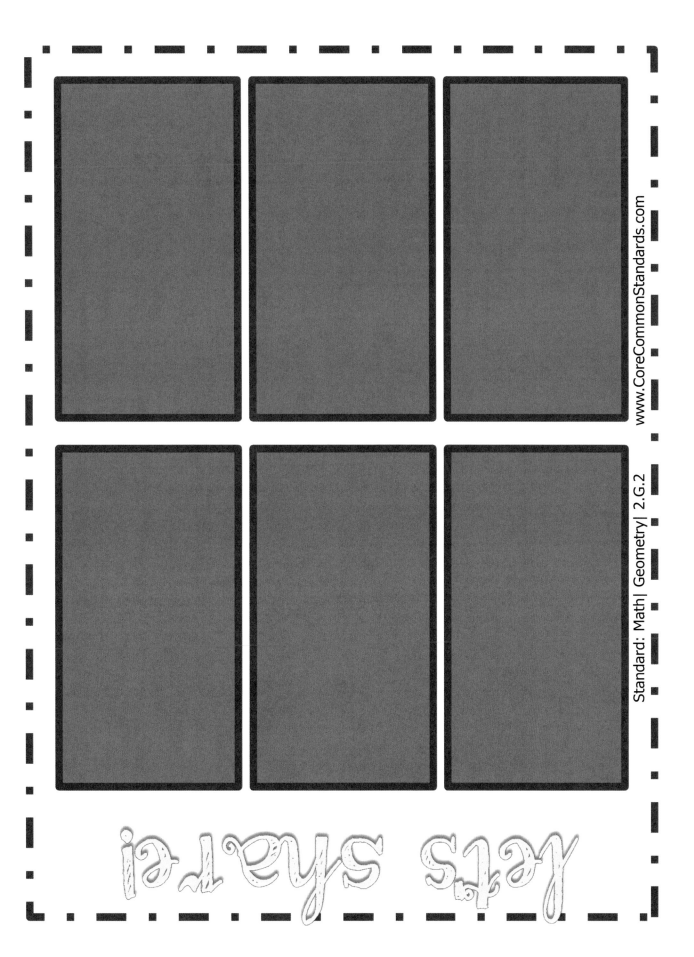

Standard: Math| Geometry| 2.G.2

Let's share!

This is a Blank Page

You May Cut Out Resources On Back

This is a Blank Page

Name: _____

cut the chocolate bars into pieces

6	5	3
10	7	9
2	4	8

Standard: Math| Geometry| 2.G.2   www.CoreCommonStandards.com

This is a Blank Page

You May Cut Out Resources On Back

This is a Blank Page

pizza for all!!!

Directions:

Partition circles and rectangles into two, three, or four equal shares; describe the shares using the words halves, thirds, half of, a third of, etc., and describe the whole as two halves, three thirds, four fourths. Recognize that equal shares of identical wholes need not have the same shape.

Mix the Fraction Activity Picture Cards into a pile. Draw a Picture Card. Each player must use their Pizza Worksheet to draw the fraction shown on the Picture Card. The first student to successfully draw the fraction on their Pizza Worksheet gets a Pizza Reward Card for that fraction. Laminate the Pizza Worksheets and use a marker for extended use

Standard: Math| Geometry| 2.G.3
www.CoreCommonStandards.com

Graphics by Scrappin Doodles

This is a Blank Page

You May Cut Out Resources On Back

This is a Blank Page

fraction
Part of a whole

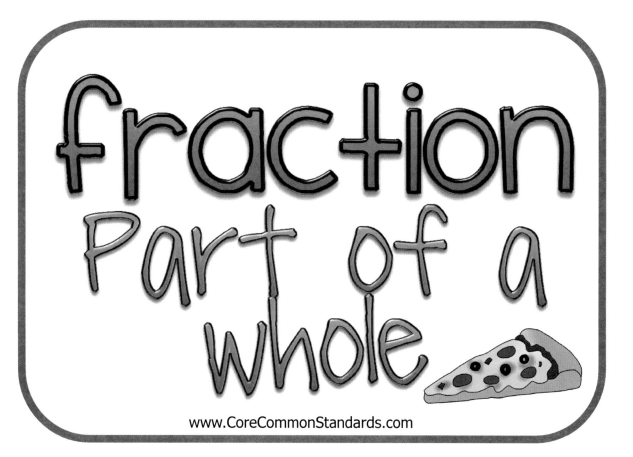

www.CoreCommonStandards.com

half

1	2

www.CoreCommonStandards.com

This is a Blank Page

You May Cut Out Resources On Back

This is a Blank Page

third

1	2	3

fourth

1	2	3	4

This is a Blank Page

You May Cut Out Resources On Back

This is a Blank Page

pizza for all!!!

With your partner, race to make a pizza the size of the fraction on the card.

If you finish first you keep the card!

First one to have 5 cards wins!

This is a Blank Page

You May Cut Out Resources On Back

This is a Blank Page

my pizza
rewards!

winner!

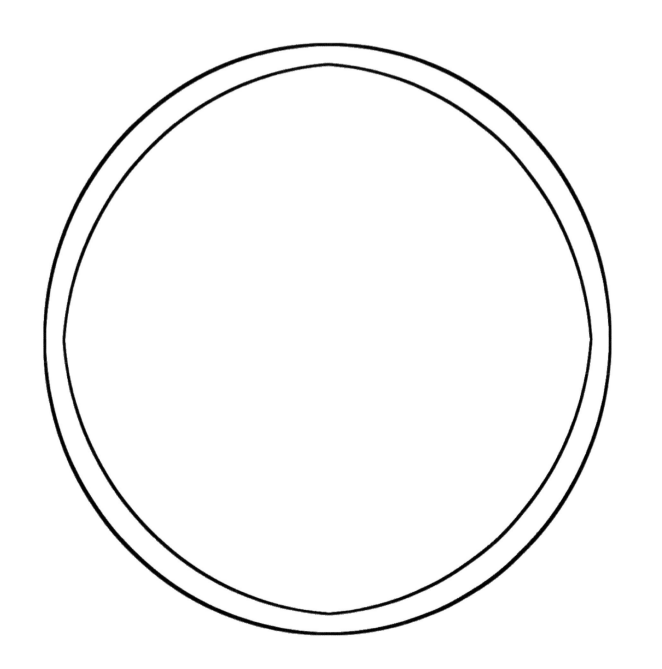

This is a Blank Page

You May Cut Out Resources On Back

This is a Blank Page

fourth

fourth

fourth

third

third

third

half

half

half

This is a Blank Page

You May Cut Out Resources On Back

This is a Blank Page